# WALKING IN THE DORDOGNE

## ABOUT THE AUTHOR

Janette Norton has lived in the Geneva region for over 30 years, raising four children and working in the marketing and educational fields. Her love of walking and exploring the mountains dates from the time she was a guide in Switzerland in her twenties. The proximity of both the Alps and Jura to her home has enabled her to continue her passion for walking. After writing her first book, on the Haute Savoie, she has moved further afield to explore other areas of France, such as Provence, the Cevennes and the Dordogne. The author's website is at www.janette.freesurf.fr.

# WALKING IN THE DORDOGNE

31 Walks in the Périgord Noir (around Sarlat)
and the Périgord Poupre (around Bergerac) including
Rocamadour and the Gouffre de Padirac in the Lot

by
**Janette Norton**

2 POLICE SQUARE, MILNTHORPE, CUMBRIA LA7 7PY
www.cicerone.co.uk

© Janette Norton 2004
ISBN 1 85284 415 9
A catalogue record for this book is available from the British Library.

## ACKNOWLEDGEMENTS

All my books have been written with the help of stalwart friends, many of them the same ones who helped me accomplish my other publications in the Haute Savoie, Provence and the Cevennes. Some have come from England, others from my home town, Geneva, some from even further afield, and I would like to thank them for their continuing support and encouragement: Alasdair Andrews, Marcelle Breton, Loulou Brown, Graham Green, Pamela Harris, Jill Heard, Janet Locke, Lynn Mermagen, Anne Nicholson, Cheryl Roberts, Jill Robson, Jill Robinson, Lorraine Ruffing and Alexa Stace, together with my sister Julia Jamison and husband, Alan, and my brother Martin Leeming and his wife, Catherine.

A special thanks to my husband, Alan, who accompanied me on many of the walks and did hours of work drawing the maps on his computer; and to my four grown-up children for criticism and advice, especially my eldest daughter, Rebecca, for helping me with the photography.

I am extremely grateful for the information and documentation provided by the various regional Tourist Offices and also from the Direction de l'Aménagement et du Développement Local – Service de l'Environnement.

### ADVICE TO READERS

While every effort has been taken to ensure the accuracy of this guidebook, readers are reminded that changes may occur rapidly in any area, which could make some contents incorrect. It is advisable to check locally on transport, accommodation and opening times of museums and chateaux.

The author would be glad to hear of any modifications such as new sign-posting or diverted paths. Please write or email Janette via the publisher, Cicerone Press. Further information on walks and updated walk directions are available on the author's website at www.janette.freesurf.fr.

*Front cover:* Medieval village of Beynac (walk 8)

# CONTENTS

# Map Key

| | |
|---|---|
| ══════ | Motorway |
| ▬▬▬▬ | Walk route (on road) |
| ▬ ▬ ▬ ▬ | Walk route (on path or track) |
| ═════ | Other road |
| - - - - - | Other path or track |
| ━━┼━━ | Railway line |
| ⌒ | River or stream |
| ☆ | Viewpoint |
| ✕ | Bridge |
| 〜 | Cliffs |
| ⌂ | Church |
| ▥ | Château |
| ⌂ | Watermill |
| ⊞ | Cemetery |
| 🐎 | Riding centre |
| △ | Camping site |
| P | Parking |
| → | Direction arrow |
| ■ | Building |
| ● | Motorway junction |

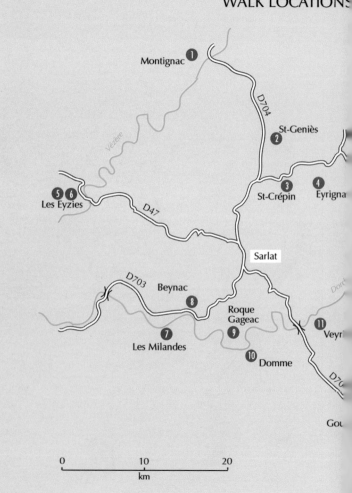

# WALK LOCATIONS

Montignac ❶

D704

St-Geniès ❷

❸ ❹
St-Crépin  Eyrigna

Vézère

❺ ❻
Les Eyzies

D47

Sarlat

Dorc

D703  Beynac

❽

Roque
Gageac

❶❶
Veyr

❼
Les Milandes

❾

❿
Domme

D70

Gou

```
0          10          20
           km
```

## (Périgord Noir)

# WALK LOCATIONS IN THE BERGERAC RE
## (Périgord Poupre)

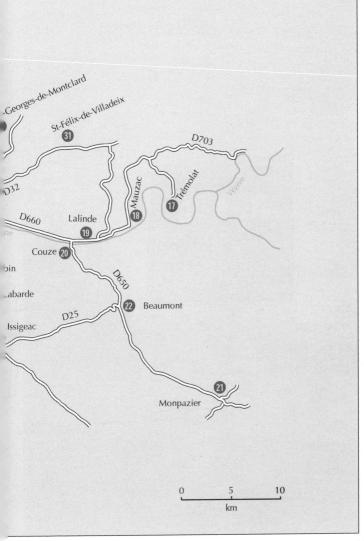

St-Georges-de-Montclard

St-Félix-de-Villadeix

**31**

D703

D32

Mauzac

Trémolat

Lalinde

**18**

**17**

D660

**19**

ne

Couze **20**

bin

D650

abarde

**22** Beaumont

Issigeac

D25

**21**

Monpazier

Vézère

| 0 | 5 | 10 |

km

*Church with traditional bell tower, Conne-de-Labarde (walk 24)*

# PREFACE

For this expatriate, who hasn't lived in England for over 35 years, visiting the Dordogne region of southwest France is like a homecoming. Gone are the towering, snow-clad peaks framing the shore of my adopted Geneva, and instead my eyes take in low rolling hillsides, lush green fields lined with hedges, snug little villages which look as if they haven't come alive since the Middle Ages and majestic châteaux, where one can imagine the clash of armour and pawing of horses as French knights rode out to meet the English in the skirmishes of the 14th-century Hundred Years' War. Winding through this placid landscape is the Dordogne river, one of the great waterways of France, now silent apart from the loudspeakers on the tourist cruises as they point out the historical sites, but once heaving with barges transporting goods down to the coast and city of Bordeaux.

When the idea of writing a walking book on the Dordogne region was first suggested to me I hesitated, as it didn't offer the challenge of high mountains and wilder places that I enjoy. Curiosity got the better of me, however, and I decided to take a look at a part of France that I had never visited, but had read so much about in historical novels featuring Eleanor of Aquitaine and her son Richard the Lionheart.

To my surprise I was enchanted by the rolling, cosy countryside, the shallow valleys ringed with trees, and the tiny hamlets and villages with beautifully restored houses surrounded by lovely gardens and often dominated by a château. I was fascinated as I walked the cobbled

*Typical Dordogne countryside*

*Walking towards the village of Phenix (walk 25)*

streets of the fortified *bastide* towns in the Bergerac region, some built by the English, others by the French, each with their central square ringed by ancient buildings. There is a certain opulence here as second-home owners and retirees have made the Dordogne a sought-out place to live. In summer the medieval villages clinging to the banks of the Dordogne are swarming with tourists, and the road along the river is clogged with traffic. But to counter this there are countless delightful little hotels and restaurants and many interesting historical sites to visit.

Here, as in most places, the crowds rapidly fall away when you start walking, and you are soon alone. Although the walking in this guide is less challenging than in high mountain areas, choosing the route has been far more difficult. When you walk in the mountains there is usually only one way to go, but in the Dordogne one walk can have many

alternative possibilities as you drift in and out of shallow valleys, cross innumerable narrow roads, stroll through hamlets and stumble on isolated chapels and shrines. Every walk is a fascinating historical discovery as you wander through this restful countryside, unaware of what may be round the next corner. Happily most of the walks are well signposted.

I first saw the Dordogne river unexpectedly in the early evening when the sun hung low and heavy in the sky. There was not a breath of wind and the willows on the banks of the river were mirrored in the shimmering metallic waters – all was silent and peaceful. Strangely, it reminded me of my childhood in a village not far from the slow-moving Thames – yes, I decided, I could write a book about this area, it gives me a cosy feeling of coming home!

*Janette Norton, 2004*

# INTRODUCTION

Both the nature and extent of the Dordogne region are difficult to define. To some people 'the Dordogne' means a river which traverses one of the most beautiful landscapes in the country, its banks dotted with medieval villages and castles, built and fought over by the English and French in the Hundred Years' War; to others it means a region in southwest France east of Bordeaux. But where its boundaries are remains rather vague. It is both these things, and for some English people it is their second home; a land which resembles England when it was peaceful and unspoilt, with no big, bustling towns and motorways clogged with traffic. The Dordogne is a land of milk and honey where you can eat delicious food and drink well-known wines at a fraction of the cost at home, while basking under a sun which lacks the intensity of that in southern France.

To be precise, the Dordogne *département*, which was created after the Revolution in 1790, lies in the administrative region of Aquitaine, a former duchy and kingdom in southwest France. It corresponds to the old province of Périgord and is the third largest *département* in the country. It covers 9222km², and is traversed by three rivers (the Domme, L'Isle and the Dordogne) flowing from the Massif Central in the northeast to the Atlantic in the southwest.

The Dordogne has four distinct regions: the Périgord Vert (green) in the north, the Périgord Blanc (white)

*Bridge over Dordogne river (walk 9)*

in the centre, the Périgord Noir (black) to the southeast and the Périgord Poupre (purple) to the southwest. To the north are the Charente and Haute-Vienne *départements* with the larger cities of Angoulême and Limoges. To the south are the Lot and Garonne, lying in another region which is a sleepy mixture of small medieval towns and unspoilt countryside. To the west is the flat fertile countryside of the Gironde with the bustling city of Bordeaux, and to the east are the wild uplands of the Massif Central. Although not in the exact centre of the country, the region could be called the heart of France, and it is certainly the most romantic!

The **Périgord Vert** in the north is a tranquil landscape of greenery, which remains green even in the driest of summers due to its humid climate. It

*Medieval window, Sarlat*

is traversed by countless rivers and torrents tumbling down from the nearby Massif Central to converge on the River Domme winding its way southwards to join the Dordogne at the town of Libourne near Bordeaux. Less well known than its southern counterparts, the Périgord Vert forms part of the Périgord/Limousin Regional Nature Park. Comprising 1800km², and created in March 1998, the park offers a wide variety of natural habits, with marshy areas, lakes and forests, together with large numbers of flora and fauna. The only town of note in the region is Notron, which has been famous for knife making since the 15th century. Notron knives, in various shapes and sizes, have been used all over the world and have their very own signature, namely an upside down V marked with three dots – there is even a knife festival every summer!

Further south is the **Périgord Blanc**, so called because of the whiteness of its limestone plateaux interspersed with poplar, oak and stunted juniper bushes. Here is the medieval town of Périgueux, the capital of the Dordogne *département*. Sitting in a lush valley on the L'Isle river, it was originally a tiny settlement occupied by Gauls. Then, with the help of the Romans, it became a prosperous town called Vésone. The full history of the rise and fall of Périgueux, as it was pillaged and rebuilt through the centuries, would take too long to relate here, but during

*Bastide town of Monpazier (walk 21)*

the 16th-century Wars of Religion the town remained staunchly Catholic while its rival, Bergerac, further south, remained Protestant. During the Revolution, when France was divided into *départements*, it was named the Dordogne capital, the original idea being that it would share this status with Bergerac and Sarlat, but it never did! It is a great town to wander around, strolling down the old streets around the interesting five-domed cathedral and savouring the delights of the market, famous for its truffles, foie gras and strawberries.

The **Périgord Noir** (black) in the southeast is perhaps the best-known of the four regions, where many an Englishman has his 'castle'. It has the greatest predominance of medieval villages and castles, many on the high rocky banks of the Dordogne, which in great winding curves thrusts its way through the forests of oak, walnuts and chestnuts. This is the land where European history began – it was here in the Vézère river valley, which joins the Dordogne at Limeuil, that the first evidence of prehistoric man was found under the imposing cliffs and grottos along the river bank (see 'A short history' below). If you want to walk back into the Middle Ages, Sarlat, the main town of the Périgord Noir, is a joy to explore. Miraculously preserved through the centuries, it has a beautiful main square surrounded by 15th-century houses with meticulously carved doorways and mullioned windows. Like all medieval towns of note it suffers from a surfeit of tourists, but even the milling crowds cannot spoil the inherent beauty of its mellowed buildings and winding streets. **More information about this region can be found below in the section 'The Sarlat and Souillac regions (Périgord Noir)'.**

Last, but by no means least, is the **Périgord Poupre** (purple), the south-western region of Périgord. The colour purple, a name only recently given to the area, signifies the crushed juice of the grapes from its famous vineyards, which produce some of the best wines in France. Here is a different landscape – mainly undulating, with numerous vineyards and fields of tobacco, maize and cereal crops, with the Dordogne, now wider and calmer, drifting gently through on its way westward to the Atlantic.

This is also the country of the *bastide* towns, which were a new concept of town building during the 14th century and answered a need for accommodation as the population expanded. The *bastides* were often constructed round an existing edifice such as a church or château. Fortified by gates and ramparts, the streets were laid out at right angles, converging on the main square and covered market place which was the centre of commerce and activity. Each settler could buy two plots, one for building and the other for cultivation, but they had to adhere to the laws of the Bailiff who represented the King of the *bastide*. He settled disputes and levied taxes, while representatives of the population were in charge of administration. The settlers had certain privileges, in that they were granted political asylum and were exempt from military service (this was important as soldiers had to spend seven years serving their country) and

inheritance laws. These little towns remain remarkably untouched and are a pleasure to visit, although you will not find yourself alone!

The main town in the Périgord Poupre is Bergerac, founded in the 12th century and built on the banks of the Dordogne. It was the first place to have a bridge over the river and was an important economic centre for the entire region, especially its port, which was the scene of bustling activity when the only means of transporting goods from up-country to Bordeaux was by boat. It was actually conquered by the English during the Hundred Years' War but repossessed by the French 50 years later. In the 16th century it was a hot-bed of Protestantism and was called the French Geneva for its strong religious convictions. However, when the Edict of Nantes was revoked in 1685, many of the wealthier merchants preferred to flee to safer countries, and this spelt a decline in the prosperity of the town.

Now prosperous once again, the town is a vibrant modern centre, yet it still retains its original old quarter, which is much appreciated by the many tourists who wander the cobbled streets, admiring the lovingly restored houses. Many come to see the small statue of Cyrano de Bergerac, the intrepid cavalier with the long nose immortalised in a recent film – what the tourists don't know is that Cyrano never set foot in the town, so why he is there is an enigma!

Bergerac is also the capital of the tobacco industry and houses the National Tobacco Museum, the only one of its kind in the country. **More information about this region can be found in the chapter 'The Bergerac region (Périgord Poupre)'.**

## THE DORDOGNE RIVER

Although the Dordogne is not the largest waterway in France, it is arguably the most beautiful and has more history along its banks than all the others. Its source stems from the meeting of two tiny streams, the Dor and the Dogne, erupting as waterfalls on the slopes of the volcanic Puy de Sancy in the Auvergne (a region north-east of the Dordogne *département*). It soon becomes a gushing stream flowing through the ski resort of Mont-Dore to carve its tumultuous and sinuous 490km journey across France to meet the Dronne and Isle rivers at Libourne near the city of Bordeaux.

And what a journey! The river first flows through the Gorges d'Avèze and the volcanic Auvergne before reaching the lake of Bort, where it is tamed by a succession of five large dams built between 1935 and 1957, each an engineering marvel and together producing over a 1000 kilo-watts of electricity a year. The river then precipitates itself through the Corrèze gorges to pierce the upland plateaux and valleys of Quercy (now the Lot). By the time the Dordogne reaches the *département* named after it the waters are wider and calmer, though the river still curls through the countryside in a series of incredible bends (the larger ones named *cingles*) and only straightens out when it reaches the rich plains around

*La Gratusse rapids, near Lalinde (walk 19)*

*Dordogne river near Creysse with gabare (near Lalinde, walks 18/19/20)*

Bergerac. Various rivers flow into it, the principal ones being the Cére, the smaller Bave and Couze from the south, and the Vézère from the north. The river formed an important frontier during the 14th-century Hundred Years' War as the English and French built and then fought over the castles and fortified towns which rose along its banks, many of them in strategic positions on high rocky cliffs with extended views over the surrounding countryside.

From earliest times the river was the only means of transport in the region, roads being almost non-existent. Chestnut, oak, beech, maple and hornbeam from the huge forests of the upper reaches of the river were floated down the river or carried on smaller boats called *gabarots*. These fragile boats were broken up when they arrived at Libourne as no water

traffic could make the return journey beyond Souillac.

At the port of Souillac the wood was loaded onto large flat-bottomed boats called *gabares* (see walk no.18). These then made the often perilous journey down to the the port of Libourne (founded by the English in 1268), near Bordeaux, where the wood was used for ship building and making wine barrels. The boats then returned loaded mainly with salt but also coffee and sugar. The *gabariers*, as the boatmen were called, had to be skilled navigators as the Dordogne was not (and still isn't) an easy river to navigate, with its flooding from sudden storms and tricky shallows and rapids. A canal was built in the mid-1880s to circumvent the trickiest and most dangerous stretch of rapids near Lalinde (the Saut de Gratusse), where special pilots guided the boats through the waters. Nevertheless, many boats broke up and crews perished as they attempted to negotiate their clumsy boats through these hazards. For part of the year the water level was not high enough for the boats to pass through, so arrival and departure times had to be carefully worked out. Often the boatmen were forced to return to Souillac on foot!

Unfortunately, the coming of the railway in the late 1800s finished this colourful but precarious way of life for ever, as it was far easier to transport the goods by rail. The rivermen vainly fought this modern means of transport, even blowing up the railway bridges built across the river.

The Dordogne is a richly historical region (see 'A short history', below), and many of the walks start from medieval sites, castles and *bastide* towns. In such cases additional background information is given in the walk description, but for more details, including places to stay and eat out, etc, the following books are recommended.

- *Southwest France* (Dordogne Lot Bordeaux), Dana Facaros and Michael Pauls (Cadogan Press)

- *The Rough Guide to the Dordogne and The Lot*, Jan Dodd (Rough Guides)

- *Dordogne,* Joy Law (Pallas). For a more in-depth study of the region.

- *Three Rivers of France (Dordogne, Lot, Tarn)*, Freda White. First published in 1952 it is a classic travel

book of the region – now somewhat out of date.

- *Discover Périgord*, translated from the French and available in local book shops in the Dordogne (MSM).

- *Le Guide Vert to Périgord/Quercy,* translated from the French (Michelin Editions du Voyage)

For French readers there is a wonderful triology of books by Christian Signol, entitled *La Rivière Espérance,* which vividly evokes the hard life of the sailors who navigated the Dordogne in the days before the railway destroyed their livelihood. These books were made into a popular French TV film.

## THE PÉRIGORD NOIR (WALKS 1–16)

The Périgord Noir was chosen as one of the two main walking areas for this guide because it is the most scenic and frequented of the four Dordogne regions. Many of the 16 walks start from picturesque villages situated on the banks of the Dordogne and Vézère, either beneath or on top of towering cliffs, thus affording the walker extensive views of the waterway meandering through multicoloured fields of crops and vineyards; others start from isolated hamlets or small châteaux. Most of them go through typical Périgord Noir countryside, which is an undulating landscape of deciduous woodland, oak truffle woods, shallow valleys, streams with ancient mills, fields of wheat and tobacco, narrow roads and quaint little villages.

To do the walks I based myself in a small house a few kilometres from Salignac-Eyrignac, 19km northeast of Sarlat. Salignac is an unpretentious village but does rate a mention in the Michelin Guide to Périgord as it is dominated by a picturesque medieval château surrounded by ramparts. The building dates from the 12th to the 17th centuries and has for centuries belonged to the powerful Salignac family (once owners of the larger Château de Fénelon – see walk no.11). The château can only be visited during July and August, 10.00–12.00 and 14.00–18.00. It has some interesting Renaissance furnished rooms.

Not far from Salignac are three of my favourite walks, namely the Gardens of Eyrignac (no.4), the walk from St-Crépin to Carlucet (no.3) and a walk around St Geniès (no.2).

The Gardens of Eyrignac are somewhat unusual in that, instead of a riot of colour, you get an eyeful of greenery – in fact, apart from a small rose garden, there are very few flowers. What makes this garden popular with visitors from all over the world is that it is an example of true French horticulture, namely exquisitely sculptured hedges, alleys and borders of deciduous and evergreen trees and bushes – a delight to see, especially when the evening sun casts shadows from green avenues over the meticulously kept lawns. More information and visiting times can be found in walk no.4.

Although featured in a number of French films, the miniature Manor de Lacypierre at St-Crépin (walk no.3) was a real find. Only 4km from Salignac and situated in an attractive

*Cariotte above Beynac (walk 8)*

Typical Dordogne house
(walk 8)

dip, it has been beautifully restored by its devoted owner who had the kindness to show me around. He found it partially ruined and used as a pigsty when he fell in love with it and bought it. It has taken many years and lots of money to restore the building to its present state and there is a fascinating exhibition of how the restoration was achieved. The short walk round the surrounding countryside is well marked and easy to follow.

If you want to see a really unspoilt village then St Geniès (walk no.2), 14km north of Sarlat, is the place to stroll through. It is mentioned in the Michelin guide as one of the most beautiful villages in the Périgord Noir region though, as there is a car park at the entrance to the village, I suspect there are lots of visitors in the summer months. The houses are ochre coloured with roofs covered with the traditional stone *lauze* tiles. There is a 12th-century church and a château. The walk starting from the village is reasonably long (14km) but well worth the effort.

If you want to get a feel of the landscape first inhabited by prehistoric man then the two walks from Les Eyzies on the Vézère river (walks 5 and 6) are a must. In each case there is a visit to a prehistoric site, one halfway round the walk (see individual walks for further information).

Montignac, also on the Vézère river north of Les Eyzies, sprung to fame when the nearby Lascaux caves were discovered (walk no.1 and 'A short history' for further information).

The caves have to be visited to really get the feel of what prehistoric man, with his limited resources, achieved artistically. The walk is 11km and can be combined with a visit to the caves. It is advisable to go out of season as there is a long wait for a guided visit and you cannot go independently.

Walks 7–11 all start from villages on or near the Dordogne and are all linked with a visit to a château, medieval village or museum. Since none of the walks are too long or strenuous (average 3 hours) there is plenty of time to explore, preferably after you have walked! This is an area where you will see the traditional maypoles (called *mai* in French): long poles stuck up near a house or in the centre of a village, their tops decked with ribbons and greenery. They are constructed to celebrate a marriage, birth or the election of the house owner to the Mairie (village council). From La Roque-Gageac (walk no.9) you can take a trip down the Dordogne on a traditional *gabare* (see 'The Dordogne river' above), past the tall cliffs of Marqueyssac château with its typical french garden of boxwood hedges.

Finally six walks have been included that are not strictly in the Dordogne region, but just over the border in the Lot. The short walk up and along the Roc de Monges cliffs south of the quaint village of St-Sozy (walk no.12) gives some of the best views of the Dordogne river and surrounding country. The Circle round

Mont Mercou (walk no.13) begins from the attractive medieval village of Martel which has seven towers and an old covered market. The site of the Gouffre de Padirac, one of the largest chasms in France, is the start of walk no.14 and if the Gouffre is open (see times at the start of the walk) you should calculate an hour for the visit. You also walk across a *causse* (flat open area), through the 15th-century fortified village of Loubressac and along a dramatic ridge – one of the most scenically varied and interesting walks in the book. Next is the impressive walk through the Alzou Gorge, with its ruined mills, to the famous and much visited shrine of Rocamadour, which was one of the most important pilgrimages in the Middle Ages (walk no.15). The sudden view of the village houses clinging to the rock face, dominated by the Basilica, is breathtaking. Finally there is walk no.16 in the picturesque Bleou valley, starting from the ancient chapel of Notre-Dame-des-Neiges near the small town of Gourdon, an unpretentious market town perched on a small bluff dominated by castle ruins.

The directions for the above walks are from Souillac, considered the gateway to the Périgord Noir region and once an important port. It is now a rather uninteresting town but does have one of the finest Romanesque churches in the region, the church of Ste-Marie, which was built when the Protestants destroyed the former church of St Martin during the Religious Wars. It has some beautiful, rather heathen looking carvings and a magnificent domed nave.

## THE PÉRIGORD POUPRE (WALKS 17–31)

There is quite a contrast between the Périgord Noir, a region of woods and shallow valleys, and its neighbour to the west, the Périgord Poupre.

Purple Périgord, south of the town of Bergerac, is an open undulating country, a land where vineyards stretch to the horizon while the Dordogne river, now wider and gentler, meanders lazily through vines and meadowland, its banks fringed with willow and wild acacia trees. Here you find the enchanting fortified *bastide* towns and countless picturesque hamlets with their distinctive churches topped by a wall of bells (*clochers-murs*).

I found a dear little cottage in the village of Monbazillac not far from the huge château; a few metres from the front door grow rows of vines from which the well-known sweet Monbazillac white wine is made. Just down the path there is a magnificent view over Bergerac and surrounding country as the castle is built on a ridge and can be seen for miles around. One of my favourite walks starts from the château and takes the walker down the gentle ridge slope and through the neighbouring vineyards, the impressive walls always visible on the horizon. Don't stop for too many *dégustations gratuites* on the way round as it is a good idea to visit the castle afterwards, where there is also free wine tasting with a choice of all the region's vintages.

Old houses in Bergerac

*Street in village of Issigeac (walk 23)*

The walks, along the river or rather above it, have been chosen to provide maximum views. Two of the walks, namely the Trémolat Horseshoe (no.17) and around the Cliffs of Mausac (no.18) show the walker how the Dordogne does a huge U-shaped turn (*cingle* in French) through the flat fertile countryside. Couze to the Château de Lanquais (no.20) gives an insight into the flourishing paper mills which once made the River Couze known far and wide. One of the mills is still operating, producing paper made in the traditional way, and the owners are proud to show you how they do it. This walk is relatively short so you can visit the Château Lanquais on the way round. The walk around Lalinde (no.19) takes in a stretch along the canal, built in the 18th century to enable the barges to circumvent the treacherous La Gratusse rapids.

Four walks have been specially chosen to give a feel of the tranquil pastoral landscape of this region, namely Conne-de-Lambarde (no.24), the circuit of St Aubin (no.25), walks around Flaugeac and Singleyrac (no.27) and Monestier (no.29). These start in sleepy little villages and take the walker through open meadowland, wide fields of wheat, barley and tobacco, in and out of woodland, over rivulets and streams and through silent hamlets where time seems to have stood still for centuries. You marvel that there are still places which have been bypassed by the rush and bustle of modern life – even in the height of summer you will see few, if any, tourists.

Not so for the popular *bastide* towns of Monpazier (no.21), Beaumont (no.22), Issigeac (no.23) and Eymet, which you pass through to do the easy walk round the recently made lac de L'Escourou (no.28). These little towns are a must to visit. At all times of the year you will find tourists sitting in the shady cafés, browsing in the trendy shops, visiting the Romanesque churches and marvelling that such beauty could have survived through the centuries. But few bother to step outside the mellowed walls of the village and explore the surroundings, so once again you will be alone in a countryside steeped in history.

The area immediately north of Bergerac is less known but no less lovely – it has a more enclosed, greener landscape with lots of woodland and smaller fields. The two small villages where the walks begin, namely St-Georges-de-Monclard (no.30) and St-Félix-de-Villadeix (no.31) are typical examples of Périgord villages, beautifully restored but uncontaminated by mass tourism. If I moved to the Dordogne, I would move here!

## A SHORT HISTORY OF THE DORDOGNE

European history began in the Dordogne region; the earliest traces of primitive man have been found in rough rock shelters on the banks of the Vézère river in the Périgord Noir and are a fascinating witness to how the earliest inhabitants (first the Neanderthals and later the Cro-Magnon) used rough flint and stone tools to carve out their dwellings and to make incredible artistic cave paintings depicting the animals they hunted and their mode of living in the

27

Beynac castle (walk 8)

harsh environment of over 10,000 years ago (see walk nos. 1, 5 and 6). Over the next few generations these nomadic hunters became settled communities tending the soil and planting crops. The Iron Age blossomed in 700BC with the arrival of the Celts, a disorganised group of many clans who built primitive towns and fortresses called 'oppida'. It was the Pétrocores (a Celtic tribe) who established an 'oppidum' on the banks of the river L'Isle which was later to become the town of Vesunna (Périgueux).

When the Romans arrived and conquered southern France during 59–51BC they brought with them law and order, building new towns and roads, and planting crops and vineyards. In AD16 the Emperor Augustus established the province of Aquitaine, which at that time extended over most of southwestern France. For three centuries there was peace and the region flourished, but it was not to last.

Roman dominance crumbled as the Visigoths and then the Franks invaded and devastated the area. In the 10th century feudalism was established and the four Périgord baronies of Mareuil, Bourdeilles, Beynac and Biron were established. In 1137 Eleanor of Aquitaine, the beautiful only daughter of the Duke of Aquitaine, inherited the duchy and, by marrying Henry of Anjou (her second husband) who in 1154 became Henry II, brought the whole of Aquitaine under English rule. This meant that the English king held sway over as much of France as the French king himself. Although the economy flourished at this time the region was plundered by Eleanor's third son, Richard the Lionheart, causing further discontent between the two countries that sowed the seed of the later Hundred Years' War.

Between 1337 and 1453 the French and English fought bitterly over the Aquitaine region in a series of battles, which culminated in the famous Battle of Castillon in 1453 when the English were finally beaten. The heroine who rallied the dispirited French soldiers to victory was a young girl called Jean d'Arc who remains a

*Medieval tower, Issigeac (walk 23)*

national heroine to the present day. It was during this time that the renowned *bastide* towns were created in the Dordogne area, some constructed by the English, others by the French, representing a sort of architectural rivalry between the two opponents (see 'Périgord Poupre', above, for further information on *bastides*).

The Religious Wars starting in the 1500s were the next disruption as Protestantism made inroads in the area and set one city against the other. Catholics rose up to protest against the new thinking and bitter battles ensued between the different towns for religious dominance. These ructions continued for almost 30 years until the Edict of Nantes in 1598 gave Protestants the same freedom to worship and hold office as the Catholics. To this day Bergerac still has a large Protestant population and place of worship (the Temple), whereas Périgueux and Sarlat have always remained staunchly Catholic. The Great Plague in 1720, which hit other areas such as Provence and decimated the population, did not make great inroads into the Dordogne, nor did the French Revolution in the late 1700s have such a dramatic effect as it did on places closer to the capital. Although many châteaux and churches were plundered, the ruling gentry were often able to flee or hide without being captured. It was after the Revolution that Aquitaine was split into different *départements* and the Département

de la Dordogne was created (see 'The Dordogne river', above).

When Napoleon Bonaparte seized power in a *coup d'état* in 1799, the Dordogne and Lot regions were very supportive of the new regime and supplied many military leaders and soldiers, but the economy was hard hit, especially in Bordeaux, when trade with Britain was prohibited in 1807.

The real change came with the Industrial Revolution and the arrival of the railway in 1851, although this was later coming to the Dordogne than to other areas. This could have been because trade was already flourishing as the large *gabares* transported goods up and down the river. When the Canal latéral was opened, joining the Garonne with the Canal du Midi, it meant that boats could get from the Mediterranean to the Atlantic – nowadays a line of transport used by tourists rather than commercial enterprises.

Towns such as Bordeaux and Périgueux continued to flourish in the 1900s, but life in the rural communities did not change. Development suffered a setback when the first appearance of the deadly phylloxera disease hit the extensive vineyards around Bergerac in 1868 – it was then that many farmers turned to growing the tobacco for which this area is also noted. The First World War halted expansion and changed the rhythm of rural life irrevocably as thousands of French peasants left to perish in the north of France. This exodus continued during the Depression in the 1930s, and the population was further depleted by the Second World War. In common with other parts of France, the Dordogne was part of the Resistance Movement against the German Occupation and, because of its relative isolation, many fighters came to the remoter areas to hide. Many atrocities occurred as villages were burnt and partisans murdered by the Germans. These difficult times are

*Château de Biron,*
*near Monpazier (walk 21)*

still etched in the memories of the older population, and monuments and plaques to the inhabitants of a village or a young Resistance group dot the countryside.

Industrialisation never came to the Dordogne after the war as it did in other areas of France – the region slumbered in pastoral decay as more and more of the small farmers left for pastures new; villages and hamlets fell into ruins. But if the peasants didn't want to live there, someone else did! The British rediscovered the Dordogne in the 1960s; from a trickle of enthusiasts snapping up the crumbling farms, manors and mills for a song to renovate them, it has become a deluge, as people see the area as an idyllic place to retire to or have a second home – you could say that, with the recent British invasion, the Hundred Years' War is being refought!

Although many French say that this influx has inflated property prices so that the local people can no longer afford to live there, overall it has helped the regional economy immensely. Wine and agricultural products are still the main regional exports, but tourism is a major money spinner as people pour in to wander round the unspoilt villages, visit the historically interesting châteaux and taste the delicious regional specialities. Let us hope the culture and tradition of the Dordogne region survive this new invasion, as they have survived during previous centuries of plunder and change.

## USING THE GUIDE

At the start of each walk details are given of the walk difficulty, time, length, maps, departure point and signposting.

### Grading

Most of the walks in this book are within the capacity of all walkers and are graded strenuous (rather than difficult), moderate and easy. The Dordogne is a country of undulating woodland and shallow valleys, so there are no long, steep climbs or sharp descents. The comments after the grading should give a good indication as to whether the walk is suitable for your abilities.

### Time

The timings correspond to the average walking pace of a reasonably fit person, but this is very approximate as everyone has a different rhythm. It is also important to add on plenty of time for stopping to look at the views, taking photos and for a picnic. As the Dordogne is easy walking country (many of the walks incorporate narrow roads) you can expect to walk between 3.5 and 4km per hour if there are no excessive gradients. Four centimetres on a 1:25,000 map equals 1km (for quick measuring put three fingers sideways on the map – roughly 4cm or 20mins walking).

### Length

When reading the walk details look carefully at the length of the walk and

## GUIDELINES TO WALKING IN THE DORDOGNE

- Read the walk description against a map before you go to ensure that the walk is within the capacity of all members of your party.

- Give yourself plenty of time by setting off early. If a walk has a timing of 5hrs, allow at least 2hrs extra for breaks and a lunch stop.

- Although the Dordogne is not usually as hot as the south of France, in summer you will need to take plenty of water and sunscreen.

- It is advisable not to deviate from the marked path – if there is a short-cut it is usually shown on the map.

- If you are walking alone, always tell someone where you are going.

- Do not pass any barrier indicating 'Propriété Privée' unless the walk description indicates that this is permitted.

- Even if the day looks hot and fine take waterproof clothing, as the weather can be changeable.

- Take your litter home with you.

- Do not pick the wild flowers but leave them for others to enjoy.

- Do not light matches or make a fire, especially when it has been dry.

- Remember to shut all gates and barriers you go through.

- In France remember to walk on the left-hand side of the road in order to face oncoming traffic.

whether it is mainly in the open or through woodland. None of the walks has a significant height gain, but some are longer than others, and the heat and humidity may slow you down on a hot day.

## Maps

Although each walk is accompanied by a sketch map it is recommended that you buy the listed 1:25,000 IGN maps, which are available in local shops. It is usually easier to buy them in the region rather than in the UK (though they may be available through specialist map suppliers such as Stanfords, www.stanfords.co.uk). Sometimes the local supermarkets sell them cheaper. A complete list of maps for the walks in this guide is given in Appendix A.

The numbers on each sketch map in the guide show key reference points along the route, especially where there are major changes in walk direction, and correspond to numbered sections in the text. Unfortunately some of the IGN maps, especially the Série Bleue series, are out of date or inaccurate and the jeep tracks and paths are not always shown. Where a turning mentioned in the text is not shown on the IGN map, it has, wherever possible, been included on the sketch map.

**Note**: On the sketch maps the walk route on paved roads (tarmac) is shown by two white lines dotted with red. For simplification, there is no distinction between jeep tracks, wide tracks or narrow paths, which are all indicated by small red dashes. Arrows show the direction of the walk.

## Signposting

This gives an indication of how well the walk is signposted and whether you are following a Grand Randonnée

*Bridge over the Dordogne at Bergerac*

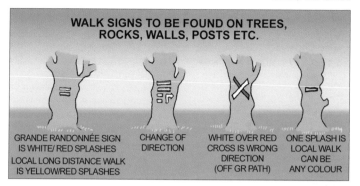

**WALK SIGNS TO BE FOUND ON TREES, ROCKS, WALLS, POSTS ETC.**

GRANDE RANDONNÉE SIGN IS WHITE/ RED SPLASHES LOCAL LONG DISTANCE WALK IS YELLOW/RED SPLASHES

CHANGE OF DIRECTION

WHITE OVER RED CROSS IS WRONG DIRECTION (OFF GR PATH)

ONE SPLASH IS LOCAL WALK CAN BE ANY COLOUR

(long-distance footpath) or a local path with its own different coloured splashes or wooden signposts.

If you see white and red horizontal paint splashes on your route you are on one of the Grandes Randonnées, which go all over France and are usually well maintained. Look at the illustrations 'Walk signs' and remember that a cross instead of a splash (of the colour you are following) means that you are about to go in the wrong direction! Some of the local walks join these paths for a while and then break away to circle back to the starting point. Local walks have different coloured splashes, but in some areas these are rather arbitrary and can suddenly disappear for no reason. In others there are so many colours that one gets bewildered!

The walks in the Dordogne area are well signposted, but it is a region criss-crossed with narrow roads, shallow valleys and little villages. Unlike mountainous regions where the way is often obvious, walking in

the Dordogne can be more difficult in terms of directions. It is wise to stick to the walk description and not try any shortcuts – you can never get seriously lost in this region, just end up in the wrong village!

**How to get there**
Just before the route description is a section 'How to get there', which gives directions to the start of each walk from a specific town (Sarlat, Souillac or Bergerac). In general the walks begin at convenient points where there is a car park or good roadside parking.

**Observations**
The observations at the start of each walk give useful additional information, which might help the reader to decide whether he or she wishes to do the walk. They also include historical background of the town or village the walk is starting from, and any anecdotes about the countryside or points of interest to be

35

seen on the way. In addition some walks include a visit to a château, museum or garden, or a boat ride – times and entrance fees are given where applicable.

## TRAVELLING TO THE DORDOGNE

### By Car

It is not possible to reach many of the walks in this book without a car. For those travelling to France by train or air, all the main car hire firms operate from stations and airports, and information about rental can be obtained from your local travel agency. In your own car the easiest route to the Dordogne (Sarlat and Bergerac) is to take the ferry or hovercraft to Calais, Dieppe or Le Havre and then to follow the motorway via Rouen, Le Mans, Tours, Poitiers, Limoges (**note:** from Poitiers to Limoges you are on the N147 as there is no motorway), Brive-la-Gaillarde and Souillac. Get off at Souillac and follow signs to Sarlat. This route avoids driving around Paris. To reach Bergerac you get off the motorway at Limoges and take the N21 to Périgueux and then Bergerac.

The motorways are refreshingly empty in France compared to Britain, except on some busy holiday weekends, and have excellent rest areas. However, there are motorway tolls to pay, which can add considerably to the cost of motoring.

There are three internet sites which will give you a detailed travel itinerary, namely www.viamichelin.com (French site), www.theaa.com/travelwatch/planner_main.jsp and www.rp.rac.co.uk/routeplanner (the official AA and RAC internet sites). These sites require as a minimum the names of two towns, but you may also add intermediate points. You can also specify fastest/ shortest route, avoiding tolls/ferries, etc.

### By Rail

The English office of the French Railways (Rail Europe, 179 Piccadilly, London W1V OBA, tel. 0870 8306030 (Brochureline) www.raileurope.co.uk) will, on request, send an informative brochure outlining the different ways to get to France by rail, including timetables, cost, car hire, travel insurance information, special hotel/rail packages for short and medium breaks, cross-channel fares, Interrail information for the under 26s, etc. For a ticket booking tel. 0870 5848848 or contact the website.

### By Bus

The most economical way to travel to the Dordogne is by bus from London's Victoria Station. For information and booking details contact Eurolines on the internet www.Eurolines.co.uk, or tel. 08705 143219 or contact your local National Express Agent.

### By Air

British Airways runs direct daily flights from London (Gatwick) to Bordeaux from March to October. It is then relatively easy to get a train to Sarlat or Bergerac. For further information contact www.britishairways.com. Ryanair has daily flights between Stanstead and Bergerac from 30th March to 25th October. For information on times and prices consult their website, www.ryannair.com.

The Dordogne climate is not extreme; it has a fairly balmy climate with mild, humid winters and long, hot summers – spring and autumn tend to be the rainy seasons. For walking it is best to go out of season, May, June, September and October being the best times. Accommodation is at a premium in July and August when the crowds arrive and prices escalate; it is often too hot to walk during these months, and there are sometimes violent thunderstorms at the end of the day. Hotels and restaurants tend to be shut in the winter season. It is very unusual to get snow in the Dordogne, although hard frosts are not unknown and the one in 1956 killed off almost all the vines. Nowadays the climate has become so capricious that one never knows what to expect at any time of year. If you like looking at the flowers, April to June are the best months, though there is usually more rain; for the autumn foliage and the *vendanges* (grape-picking), choose September to October, which is often sunnier.

## ACCOMMODATION

The Dordogne is a major tourist region and there is plenty of accommodation to choose from, ranging from first-class hotels to primitive camp sites; it is all a matter of choice and how much you want to spend.

In July and August most places are full and the camping sites are cheek by jowl. It is much easier to find accommodation in May, June, September and October when there are fewer people about and prices are lower. It is always advisable to book in advance.

Hotels in France are typically less expensive than in England and are great value – the only things missing is the hearty breakfast – you pay extra for this in a French hotel. Most rooms have en-suite bathroom or shower and WC. The choice is wide, but below are some recommended hotel chains.

**Logis de France:** This is a nationwide network of hotels that offer comfortable accommodation and excellent food at reasonable prices. The hotels are graded from one to three stars according to their degree of comfort (look for the distinctive logo – a yellow fireplace on a green background). The Logis de France book, listing all the hotels available with additional information regarding facilities, is available from good bookshops or the Maison de la France shop in Piccadilly (see below), website: www.logis-de-france.fr.

Main square in Sarlat

**Campanile Hotels:** These tend to be on the outskirts of towns rather than in villages. They are usually modern and impersonal, catering more for the family market than the discerning tourist. For further information and a free booklet (only partially in English) tel 0208 569 6969 in the UK; or tel. 01.64.62.46.00 fax 01.64.62.46.61; website: www.enver-gue.fr in France. (This website also lists other hotel chains.)

**Hotel Guidebooks:** *Guide to the châteaux and hotels de France:* If you want to go up-market there is a book published with a list of châteaux (often with the owners acting as hosts) and independent hotels available all over France. There is a description in English and a photo of each establishment. Prices of the rooms and meals are clearly marked. Some of them are not at all expensive for what they offer.

Address: 30 Rue des Jeûneurs, 75002 Paris, tel. (33) 1.55.34.16.10, reservations: (33) 1.72.72.92.02 (English spoken), website: www.chateauxhotels.com. Look for accommodation by area – online reservations.

Guidebook series of Hotels de Charme en France. Editions Rivage – also available in English. Hotels and bed and breakfast establishments all over the country. Website: www.guidesdecharme.com for all information in English and online reservations.

**Gîtes de France:** These are country cottages which are available for a weekly rent all over the French countryside and are good value. They can vary from extremely comfortable to quite basic, so read the small print beside each photo in your brochure carefully! It is a good idea to pick an area of this guide that appeals to you and then rent a *gîte* in a central position for the walks indicated. Gîtes de France holidays are now run in conjunction with Brittany Ferries. For information and booking, contact www.gites-de-France.fr/eng/index.htm. This website gives information on all types of *gîtes*, and online reservations are possible.

**Gîtes d'étape:** This is a type of youth hostel, usually with a warden, and open to people of all ages. They can be reasonably comfortable with good beds, showers and a well-equipped kitchen, but they can also be quite basic with dormitories and are mainly intended for cheap overnight stops by walkers and cyclists. Some of them offer meals, but if not there is often a café/restaurant in the vicinity. In the high season they can be uncomfortably full, but are a wonderful way to get to know fellow travellers and share a convivial evening. Out of season you often have the place to yourself. A complete guide to *gîtes d'étape* all over France is available from good bookshops, Brittany Ferries or the bookshop at Maison de la France. Website: www.gite-etape.com

**Chambres d'Hôtes:** This is the English equivalent of bed and breakfast, though often the breakfast is not included or is limited to coffee and bread (croissants if you are lucky). The number of these establishments is increasing all over France (look for the Chambre d'Hôtes sign or enquire in the local café or shop). The degree of comfort varies tremendously, and you will rarely get a TV or beverage-making facilities in your room. Most rooms have their own shower/toilet, but you could be sharing with the family.

The book *French Country Welcome* is available from the Maison de la France shop (see below). Website: www.gites-de-France.fr/eng/index.htm.

**Camping:** The Dordogne region has a number of camping sites, many of them on the banks of the Dordogne river. Camping sites are graded from one to five stars, and range from those offering a shop, hot showers and a swimming pool to sites with basic washing facilities.

*Camping à la ferme* is cheap and popular, though the facilities are minimal – remember some toilets in France, especially on camping sites, are still of the squat variety! Website: www.gites-de-France.fr/eng/index.htm.

The local Tourist Offices (see Appendix B) have a complete list of camping sites. Most of them speak English and will gladly send the information. Otherwise telephone Maison de la France (see below).

**Further information:** For more information concerning the Dordogne contact:

Maison de la France
178 Piccadilly
London WIV OAL

Tel. 09068 244123
Fax 020 7493 6594
Email: info@mdlf.co.uk
Internet: www.franceguide.com

There is also a shop selling a wide range of books in English and French. French Information Line: tel. 09068 244123 (affiliated to Maison de La France). Open 10.00–18.00 Monday to Friday, and 10.00–17.00 Saturday.

## CLOTHING AND EQUIPMENT

The Dordogne does not suffer from extreme ranges of temperature. In general summers are hotter than those in the UK, though nowadays one never knows how the weather will behave!

The best solution is to dress in light layers and, even if the weather looks good, take a windproof jacket; choose the breathable type to avoid getting hot and sweaty. When the sun shines the rays are intense, so sun protection is important, as is a shady hat. The type of trousers which zip down into shorts are very practical, as on many of the walks there are prickly gorse and broom bushes and you get quite scratched if you have bare legs.

Walking in the Dordogne is not comparable to trekking in more rugged country, and many of the walks could be done in a stout pair of training shoes with suitable soles or in special walking sandals. However, it is preferable and more comfortable to have a lightweight pair of sturdy boots with plenty of ankle support and soles that grip well on rocky terrain.

As none of the walks described is long, a light or medium-weight rucksack is quite adequate. It is wise to carry a compass, provided you know

River at Beynac (walk 8)

*Spring and lavoir deep in woods near Lalinde (walk 19)*

how to use it. A mobile telephone is also useful, but will not work in certain areas.

The following is a suggested list of essentials for your rucksack for a day's walk:

- map as stipulated in the route description

- compass

- basic first-aid kit including insect repellent

- survival blanket (useful if you get lost or hurt)

- high-factor sun cream and lip salve

- sun hat and sunglasses

- woolly hat and gloves (winter only)

- glucose tablets and/or chocolate (useful if your energy flags)

- Swiss Army knife with as many attachments as possible

- cape or poncho that goes over everything including your rucksack (useful in the rain and for sitting on)

- a lightweight sweater

- a lightweight wind- and waterproof jacket

- water bottle – **note it is essential to take lots of water if the weather is hot; do not drink from streams or dubious village fountains**

- picnic (buy a crusty baguette at the local bakery before you set off and eat it with fresh cheese or ham – so much nicer than soggy sandwiches!).

- optional extras: altimeter, camera, binoculars, mobile phone and reference books.

## REGIONAL SPECIALITIES

One cannot write any sort of book about the Dordogne without mentioning the food, and there is nothing more delightful than sitting down to a *menu de terroir* ('menu of local specialities') in a village restaurant after a long day's walk when you feel justified in being really hungry!

Périgord is one of the most important gastronomic regions in France, its most notable produce being duck, goose, truffles, mushrooms, nuts and fruits such as strawberries, plums and cherries – all accompanied by a delectable Bordeaux wine.

The renowned and delicious *foie gras* springs to mind when the gastronomic delights of Périgord are discussed. A smooth, rich paté, best eaten with slivers of toast, it is made from the enlarged livers of goose or duck. Unfortunately the method of obtaining these livers is against the principles of many people; the birds are raised in the open for around four months and then kept inside in the dark and fed with maize which is forced down their gullets by a tube. This is called the *gavage*, and although the farmers are very gentle with the birds so as not to harm the livers, it is not a pretty sight. However, my principles often fly out of the window when I see *foie gras* on the menu – and it always is!

The liver is not the only part of the bird eaten; another succulent *entrée* (starter) is *salade du gesiers*, preserved duck gizzards served warm on crisp lettuce. If you don't care for duck there is usually a nourishing soup, the traditional *tourin blanchi*. In most restaurants they serve this before the starter as an extra 'on the house'; it consists of an enormous tureen of soup, containing vegetables, bits of meat and bread laced with lots of garlic. If you eat too much of this you are full before you start!

As a main course there is nothing to beat a *confit* – the meat of the duck preserved in its own thick fat and often served with *pommes sarladaise*, consisting of fried, thickly sliced potatoes again laced with garlic. *Magret de canard* (thin grilled duck breasts) is another speciality often on the menu. You can also have duck and goose served up in sausages or *cassoulet* (a sort of meat stew with haricot beans). In fact the fat of ducks and geese is used for cooking just about everything, and it gives every dish a delicious taste.

Those who live in the Dordogne permanently often get 'ducked out', but there are alternatives such as local lamb which is raised on the nearby *causses* (upland plateaux) in the Quercy area; pork, which is often stuffed with garlic, prunes and truffles; and rabbit, served in a variety of ways.

Fish dishes do not play a major role in a Périgord menu although trout, pike, perch are fished from the rivers. Eels and lampreys are poached in wine, but are not to everyone's taste. After reading that Henry I died suddenly after eating a huge plate of lampreys in the 11th century, I have never felt a desire to try them! Nowadays a wide range of fresh sea fish from the Atlantic is available around Bordeaux.

Vegetarians can indulge themselves with the renowned Périgord black truffles (see 'Vegetation, flowers and wildlife', below), though personally I think they are overrated and expensive. Truffles are best experienced in an omelette, although they are often served in sauces. If your purse does not stretch to this expensive culinary delicacy, there are other types of mushroom which are also delicious in season, such as *morilles*, *chanterelles*, *girolles* and *bolets*.

Forget the cheese unless you like goat's cheese; the only local cheese readily available is called *cabécou* and comes from the Rocamadour region. Go straight to the deserts – the juiciest strawberries in the whole of France come from the Vergt region,

between Périgueux and Bergerac; cherry, peach and plum orchards abound, especially south of Bergerac. The fruit is often made into tarts or *clafoutis* (fruit in a light cake mixture); walnuts and hazelnuts are also made into tarts and cakes, and nut liqueur is much appreciated.

The region around Bordeaux is one of the world's greatest wine producing areas and a whole chapter could be dedicated to the different types of wine (called *appellations*) and where they are to be found. But this is a walking book and I am not even going to try! Find a wine you like and drink it is my advice, or take the house wine (*vin de maison*), which is usually served in a jug. When I stayed in Monbazillac I enjoyed the sweet, light white wine that I bought from my landlord, whose vineyards almost

*A gaggle of geese fattening in a field – Dordogne*

Traditional bake oven in a Dordogne village

came up to my front door – this is often drunk as an aperitif rather than during the meal.

Bon appetit!

## VEGETATION, FLOWERS AND WILDLIFE

The Dordogne, with its gentle climate and rainfall, is an area of abundance, and it is not surprising that the soil is host to a diversity of trees and flowers. Almost everything grows here, and there is a richness of vegetation that you do not see further south in France, where the long hot summers shrivel up the earth to a uniform brown.

Nevertheless, the different areas have a mosaic of micro-climates that favour a specific type of agriculture and flora, often a mixture of Mediterranean and temperate. On the

upper reaches of the Dordogne there are large forests of mixed deciduous trees and a flourishing logging industry. The Sarlat area is a region of limestone tree-covered hills and narrow valleys planted with cereals, maize, sunflowers and tobacco. This region, especially the southeast, is the largest tobacco producing area in France, and the walker will come across the long wooden barns where the tobacco is hung to dry, as well as the more modern plastic tunnels with motorised drying machines.

It is also a main production centre of the fabled truffle, a gastronomic delicacy second to none, and while walking you will come across oak plantations which have been fenced off from would-be predators of this precious commodity. Normally the trees are planted in rows called *truffières,* and the mushroom-like fungus is dug out from the roots by specially trained dogs or pigs and harvested in winter when it is ripe and odorous. Near to the farms you will see fields of gaggling geese and ducks as this is also *foie gras* country (see 'Regional specialities', above). In this more northeasterly area the Dordogne cliffs are covered in green oak, juniper and coniferous trees.

As the river winds towards the coast the countryside becomes flatter and the fields larger, the cereals and tobacco fields giving way to vast vineyards interspersed with fruit and nut orchards. The Périgord Poupre is particularly noted for its plums, the fruit being processed in Agen further south in the Lot. But the vineyards predominate, especially south of

Bergerac around Monbazillac, where the gentle slopes are covered in vineyards as far as the eye can see. Further south, around the *bastide* towns of Issegeac, Beaumont and Montpazier, there are fewer vines and cereals, and tobacco and dairy farms predominate. The Dordogne is also one of the biggest producers of strawberries in France, the juiciest coming from the area between Périgueux and Bergerac.

The many woodland areas, particularly in the Périgord Noir, are mainly deciduous with, among others, chestnuts, horse chestnuts, oaks, ash, walnuts, beech and hawthorn; the most striking is the false acacia with its hanging clusters of creamy flowers, a tree which is not

*Tobacco drying near Veyrines-de-Dome (walk 7)*

45

Vineyards at Château de Monbazillac (walk 26)

endemic to Europe but flourishes in this region.

## Flowers

In addition to this agricultural diversity the region hosts an abundance of flora. In springtime the wooded areas are covered in primroses, violets, periwinkles, snowdrops and white wood anemones; in the denser undergrowth, where there is less light, holly bushes, black alder, wild veronica and honeysuckle flourish. The open fields are carpeted in summer with ox-eye daisies, purple wild sage and columbines. On the river banks, by the many small ponds and streams and in the often marshy bottoms of the narrow valleys, grow the flora that love humidity, such as the delicate fritillaries, water avens, yellow irises and marsh marigolds, along with a variety of tall rushes.

The drier, sandy and stonier soil of the vineyards is host to the scarlet *Tulipa aegenensis* or *tulipes de vignes* (there does not seem to be an English translation), and dog rose bushes border the vineyards as disease protectors. On the rocky cliffs above the river bloom creeping plants such as varied species of saxifrage, stonecrop and ferns. When you walk through an area of green oak, juniper and broom bushes you know that you are in a micro-climate where Mediterranean plants, such as lavender, thyme and rosemary, are dominant.

The most exciting aspect of this area for any flower-lover is the multitude of wild orchids in the fields and woods, not just the odd specimen but huge clusters of them which have obviously multiplied and not been touched or sprayed. The red and white helleborine thrive in the shady wood-

*Pyramid orchid, near Monestier
(walk 26)*

*Lady orchid
(walk 23)*

*Tongue orchid
(walk 25)*

Woodcock orchid (walk 26)

Loose-flowered orchid (walk 30)

land as do the early purple orchids, but other varieties, such as the pyramid, man and fragrant, can be found in open grassland or on the path verges. Huge tall lizard orchids have been seen on walks 10 and 11, and the author saw a most impressive display of stately lady orchids when walking through upland country near Issegeac (walk no.23). Other discoveries were the curious purple tongue orchids, the purple loose-flowered orchids and the beguiling bee and woodcock orchids.

But perhaps the memory of the brazen crimson of the poppy meadows on the banks of the Dordogne in the Périgord Noir in early June is what most visitors to the region will remember with nostalgia.

**Suggested books**

*The Hamlyn Guide to Wild Flowers of Britain and Europe* (1992, Hamlyn),

D. and R. Aichele and H. W. and A. Schwegler. Paperback edition.

*Mediterranean Wild Flowers,* Marjorie Blamey and Christopher Grey-Wilson (1990, Harper Collins). A complete guide with over 2000 illustrations, this includes illustrations of the different pines and deciduous trees but only applies to the southern area of France. Since the Dordogne has both climates it is useful.

*Field Guide to Orchids of Britain and Europe,* Karl Peter Buttler. Consultant editor Paul Davies (1991, Crowood Press). A wonderful reference book with over 750 illustrations of every European species.

**Wildlife**

The Dordogne has a history of hunting – one can imagine the knights of old galloping out of their castles on their sturdy steeds to shoot wild boar and deer, which were plentiful centuries ago, in the vast forests. With the advent of more accurate firearms, the woods and farmlands were decimated of wildlife during the late 18th century. Nowadays, with the ecology movement sweeping the country, more animals are visible than ever before, and there is a defined hunting season.

In the forests live wild boar, foxes, badgers, rabbits, voles, squirrels and the elusive civet cats – in the higher open areas roam the hares, weasels, stoats and deer. I have happily seen no snakes here, though the common grass snake and vipers do exist. One rodent that is slowly gaining ground in the lakes and rivers is the coypu, a big furry animal rather like a beaver. It was originally introduced from South America and does not have any natural enemy except man. Measures are now being taken to eliminate these animals as, although vegetarian, their increasing numbers are destroying the riverbanks, the natural habitat of otters and water voles (see walk no.28).

Birds are everywhere, and more prevalent here than in the more southern regions of France. In the woods are thrushes, robins, nuthatch, blackbirds, coal tits and other common species, as well as woodcock and nightingales. Above the rocky cliffs of the Dordogne, cruising the thermals, are buzzards (see walk no.18), black kites and peregrine falcons, the latter only re-establishing themselves in the 1980s. The cliffs are riddled with the nests of colonies of swallows, swifts and sandmartins, especially along the Vézère river, and the dank, dark caves, once the home of primitive man, now harbour thousands of bats!

At a lower level wild ducks, coots and moorhens nest in the reeds and marshes and, if you are lucky, you can see the blue flash of a kingfisher as it skims over the water; often you see herons watching for fish, standing on one leg in the shallows. The Dordogne used to be alive with trout, salmon, eels, and the rarer turtle, but now, due to repeated over-fishing, sewage and insecticide, numbers have diminished. Recently steps have been taken to remedy this deficit and hopefully numbers will increase again.

The vineyards are home to the red-legged partridge, which we used to watch every evening from our cottage in Montbazillac as a couple picked their way leisurely through the rows of plants, scratching for insects and snails. But my favourite, and the most eye-catching bird to be seen in the Dordogne region, especially in the south, is the flamboyant hoopoe, which flies in at the end of April after wintering in Africa. His long curved beak, pink chest and pied wings are offset by a huge crest which opens up on landing to make him look like an Indian chief – it is a sight worth seeing!

Beynac cas

# WALK 1
## *Walk Around Montignac and les Caves de Lascaux*

| | |
|---|---|
| **Difficulty** | Easy, undulating walk |
| **Time:** | 3hrs 15 mins |
| **Length:** | 11.7km |
| **Map:** | Carte Série Bleu 2035 O Montignac/ Grotte de Lascaux 1:25,000. |
| | Map at the back of descriptive Circuit Pédestre No.8 available at the Tourist Bureau in Montignac. |
| **Depart from:** | Parking – modern bridge in Montignac |
| **Signposting:** | Non-existent at the start but later yellow splashes and signs Circuit Pedestre (walk no.8) |

An easy walk with pleasant open views over the Laurence and Vézère valleys. The return is 5km along a road but there is little traffic. Montignac, situated on the Vézère river, looks an unpretentious little town, but in fact it had a long history well before the discovery of the nearby Lascaux caves. From the 11th to the 14th centuries it was the key to the Périgord Noir and seat of the notorious Périgord counts. All that remains of the imposing Château de Montignac are crumbling walls and terraces and a single tower (see 2 below).

Montignac was also the home of a Eugène Le Roy, who was the author of a number of novels depicting Périgord life in the 18th century. There is a museum dedicated to his life and work near the information centre (former Hôpital St-Jean-l'Evangéliste).

### How to get there (from Sarlat)
Take the D704 signposted Montignac/Brive for 24km. When you arrive in Montignac go towards the centre of the town and park in a small parking on the right (the post office is on the left).

### Directions

1   Go out of the parking and turn right, passing the old church of St-Georges and the information centre ahead (Ancien Hôpital St-Jean). Keep going,

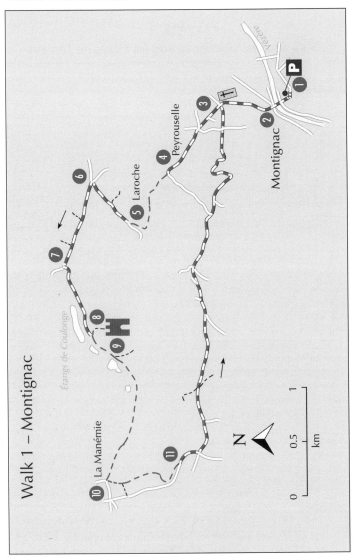

Walk 1 – Montignac

## The Lascaux Caves

The Lascaux caves were discovered in September 1944 by four local lads looking for their dog which had disappeared down a hole. On squeezing through the opening they were amazed to find themselves in a vast underground cave covered in paintings of hunting scenes. These were later verified by experts as dating from prehistoric times and of great historical interest. They were opened to the public in 1948, but due to the numbers of visitors the paintings began to deteriorate and the original caves were closed in 1963. It took 15 years for a complete fascimile (Lascaux II) to be constructed 200 metres from the original paintings.

The guided tour takes approximately 40 minutes and is also available in English. **Opening times:** April–September 9.00–19.00. October open same times but closed on Mondays. February–March and November–December 10.00–12.30 and 13.30–17.30. Closed 25th December and 1st January. **Note:** From Easter to 1st October, tickets to the cave can only be bought at the Billetterie de Lascaux in the centre of Montignac and are stamped with the time of the visit.

crossing an old bridge (constructed in 1768 under the auspices of Louis XV) over the attractive Vézère river to reach a small crossroads (10 mins).

2    Go straight up the Rue de la Liberté following the sign to Fanlac – 50m on the left is a plaque on the wall of a house commemorating the birthplace of the well-known philosopher Joseph Joubert (1754–1824), friend of Châteaubriand and Pauline de Beaumont. Further up at a sign right, Vieux Quartiers, you can see the vestiges of the imposing fortress of the Château de Montignac belonging to the Counts of Périgord and besieged in 1398 by the king's troops. On the other side of the road is an old *lavoir* (washing trough and spring). Continue up the road and out of the town, reaching a crossroads where there is a cemetery up on the right through the trees (20 mins).

3    Go straight on, signposted Périgueux/Brive, for about 200m and take the second turning left indicating Les Picadis and Circuit Pedestre No.8 (walk you are doing). Here you get your first yellow splash. This is a narrow road going up fairly steeply past the occasional house through pastures and woods to reach an area called Peyrouselle. At the top here there is a lovely extended view over the nearby shallow valley of Laurence and further over right to the famous Vézère valley (30 mins).

4    Continue to the right on a narrower road that turns into a grassy lane bordered by chestnut bushes and brambles with an old stone wall. It goes down medium steep through tall oak woods to reach a barn and an open glade where there is a walnut orchard. The track reaches a jeep track by the barn and bears right to a narrow paved road (50 mins).

5    Go down right at Laroche to another road by a house 5 mins later.

6    Go left to walk along the side of the attractive shallow valley of La Laurence with pleasant fields and a few houses scattered about on the hillsides. Keep on this road, ignoring any tracks coming in, until you reach a road left signposted to Les Memeries/Coulonge (1hr 10 mins).

7    Go up this road, and 50m later at a fork keep right towards Coulonge. The road goes into woods going gently upwards through oak and pinewoods. Over on the right through the trees you can see some ponds called Les Etangs de Coulonge, which look man made, probably for fishing. You reach the entrance of a large château (being restored in 2003) with two attractive towers each end and an impressive door in the middle (1hr 20 mins).

8    Bear down right on a jeep track (ignore track up to the left), passing one of the château towers and more ponds right to reach a walnut grove in a small field at the bottom. The track continues up again and continues straight (ignore track coming in from the right). You reach a beautiful lake surrounded by trees with a little sandy beach complete with half-sunken rowing boat – looks rather like a Monet painting. This is an excellent place for a picnic (1hr 30 mins).

9    Continue straight (do not take the jeep track up left) by a field with a small building in it. **Careful** – do not bear right to a small pond by a laurel hedge where there is 'Propriété Privé' on a tree. Go straight to enter a leafy lane to reach another big field surrounded by trees. The path goes round the field – do not enter the woods at the end but turn up left round a further field to go up gently to more woods at the top. Ignore the track coming in from the left and bear up right where there is another field sloping down on the right. As you round a corner you can see a lovely old manor house called La Manémie, property of the Royal Notaries since 1585 (1hr 55 mins).

Small lake near Montignac

**10** Just before you reach the manor house go left on a hairpin bend through open fields past two old disused barns. Further on to the left is an extended view of the peaceful, undulating, mainly wood-covered Dordogne countryside – you can see the village of Moulenèrie and the château of Coulonge passed earlier, which looks as if you have walked a long way since then! The track bears round to the left to reach a paved road (2hrs 10 mins).

**11** Go left and walk through woods to reach another crossroads, where you follow the sign 'Montignac 5km'. Go left again and keep on this road (ignoring all others coming in), which winds gently down with open views and does a final large bend at the end to reach the original crossroads you came up by the cemetery. Go right and retrace your steps into Montignac (3hrs 15 mins).

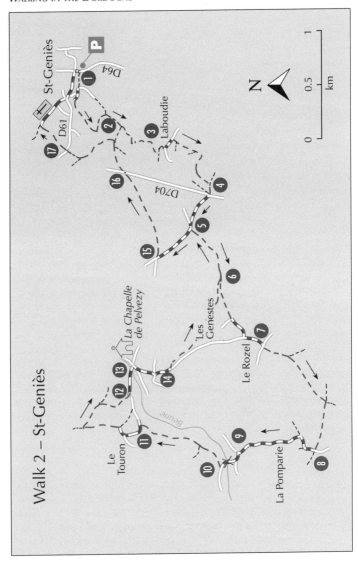

Walk 2 – St-Geniès

# WALK 2
## *Le Chemin des Combes: A Walk around St-Geniès*

| | |
|---|---|
| **Difficulty:** | Easy, undulating walk |
| **Time:** | 4hrs 15 mins plus extra time to look around the village |
| **Length:** | 14.9km |
| **Maps:** | Cartes IGN 2036 ET Top 25 Sarlat/Souillac/Vallée de la Dordogne 1:25,000 and map from Syndicat d'Initiative Salignac |
| **Depart from:** | Large parking at the bottom of the village of St-Geniès |
| **Signposting:** | Good – follow yellow splashes carefully as there is a lot of twisting and turning |

A really attractive walk around typical unspoilt Dordogne countryside far from the tourist crowds. St-Geniès is a typical Périgord medieval village with its ocre-coloured houses and roofs covered with *lauzes* (traditional grey tiles). It has a 12th-century church and 13th–16th-century château, and the imposing square tower of the 15th-century Cheylard chapel dominates the village and Chironde valley. With its quaint squares and winding cobbled streets, all tastefully restored, it is certainly worth a visit, though the churches are always shut.

### How to get there (from Sarlat)
From Sarlat take the D704 signposted Montignac/Brive La Gaillarde and continue until you see a sign right to Salignac/St-Geniès on the D60. Then turn left on the D64, direction St-Geniès, for 5km (14km from Sarlat). Park in the large parking on the right at the entrance to the village (14km from Sarlat).

### Directions

1  Go up the steps and cross the road, where you will see walking signs. Go right following sign '1, 2, 4, 5' (these are the numbers of the walks – remember yours is No.4). Almost immediately you come to a crossroads, where you turn left on the D64 and then almost immediately right on a wide track with a small park on the right, with a stream running through it and the village houses beyond. Do not take the first turning right, but pass the Salle

Abbé R.Delprat, who founded the Society of Saint Roch in 1947. This is a school of music and twirling (what sort of twirling one wonders – whirling dervishes spring to mind!). Beyond are some interesting carved doors.

The track turns to the right down a street with a high wall on the right (Chemin du Rouchou), although the name is not visible anywhere! **Careful** – at the end of the street bear to the left; this is indicated by yellow splashes but not obvious. (If you turn right and into the village proper you will be doing the walk the wrong way round!) This is a grassy path going by a house with a magnificent creeper-covered archway and there is a high wall on the right. The path comes out into fields, becoming more of a lane as it winds left and right and then left shortly after passing new houses to reach wooden signposts (20 mins).

2    Go right following a wooden sign saying '4' and walk between fields and woodland on a wide track to reach another sign indicating left. As you go along here there are lovely views over typical rolling Périgord countryside.

3    **Careful** – Turn left in front of a long, low, red building just before reaching a large farm and the hamlet of Laboudie (30 mins). The grassy path reaches a narrow road by a farm, where

*Walking through the village of St-Geniès*

you turn down left, and shortly after the sign marking the end of Laboudie turn up to the right into a chestnut wood. Keep to the main path through the wood following yellow splashes. After a few minutes the track bends round the edge of the wood and there are new houses over on the left. The track continues round the side of a field bending to the right and then plunges back into woodland again. It comes out into a field to meet the D704 (1hr).

4    Go straight across the road following yellow splash and signs La Fargeonnerie/ Trémouille and Le Rousset and walk along the road for a few minutes.

**5** Go left following a wooden sign '4A' (4B goes straight on and is a shorter way back to the beginning of the walk – you will be taking this direction on the return journey). The track goes downward through chestnut woods, continuing along the edge of the wood with a cultivated field on the left to reach another sign at the end of the field (1hr 15 mins).

**6** Go left at the sign '4A' and then after a few metres bear right. (4B, continuing straight, is where you will join from on the return, as this is the second part of the figure-of-eight walk.) The path undulates along by fields and then up a hill on a wide jeep track to reach a *ferme/auberge* (farm offering food) called Les Genestes on the right. At the farm the track becomes paved and winds down to reach a T-junction. Turn left to reach a small crossroads (1hr 25 mins). *On the right you can see the hamlet of Le Rozel, which is worth strolling into to see some unspoilt Périgord houses.*

**7** Go straight onto a jeep track which takes you through open countryside and wide fields where you have extended views in all directions. You can see a number of little hamlets on the horizon. A few minutes later the track bears right by a clump of trees and then continues through open fields with no hedges to impede the views before it starts to descend gently to further crossroads (1hr 50 mins).

**8** Turn right down towards the hamlet of La Pomparie (1hr 50 mins). At a fork by a farm keep right. The road bears round left (do not go straight on a jeep track here) and descends into the wide, shallow valley of La Beune to reach a T-junction by a weedy pond on the other side of the road (2hrs).

**9** Turn left, and shortly after the road does a wide turn right and goes over a small bridge across a narrow stream.

**10** Go up right a few minutes later on a jeep track signposted La Mouynarie (ignore another path to the left with a 'Chemin Privée' sign). This track bends back right and goes along the side of La Beune valley, slightly raised, skirting the edge of the woods and going through patches of woodland. Keep to the main track following yellow splashes to meet another narrow paved road (2hrs 20 mins).

**11** Turn left (the road surface degenerates) to reach a tumble-down hamlet called Le Touron where most of the houses need to be renovated. There is an old *four à pain* (bake-house) here which has also not yet been done up – which is somehow refreshing!

Go left just after a dilapidated barn (difficult to see but it is marked) on a wide grassy track going up out of the Beune valley; there is a lovely view if you look behind you. Follow the yellow splashes carefully as the path enters woodland again and bears down right (*proprieté privée* up to the left). The track passes a large ruined house called La Vigne on the right. Keep to the main track bearing right (do not go straight), which widens before descending to another road (2hrs 45 mins).

**12** Go left past an EDF (Electricité de France) holiday centre, where there are lots of green tents and an old building called the Château de Pelvezy with a huge tower in the middle which is an old *pigeonnier* (dovecot). You reach a crossroads where there is a dilapidated old chapel called La Chapelle de Pelvezy on the other side (2hrs 50 mins).

**13** Go right and then up left following signs to Le Mazaud, Les Farges, Le Rozel, Les Genestes. Keep on the narrow road (do not follow the sign to Le Mazaud) through woodland and fields and then look for a yellow splash on a telephone pole indicating left (2hrs 55 mins).

**14** Go down left on a grassy path into a shallow combe (small valley), which you cross, and go along the other side with the edge of the wood left and fields to the right to the signposts passed earlier (see point 7, above). *When we did this walk there were lots of lovely butterflies along here. We also*

*Church in the village of St-Geniès*

*picked tomatoes, which were falling off the plants!* Go straight on at the signpost (3hrs 10 mins) to enter the same woods taken on the outward journey (this time the path is going upwards) and reach the road you came in by from the right (see point 6). Turn left (3hrs 20 mins) and continue along until you come to crossroads.

15 Turn right (to the left is signposted La Fargeonnerie) on another wide jeep track going slightly down and passing a vineyard on the right. Continue straight (do not follow the path round to the right), entering woodland going into another shallow combe which you cross and enter woodland the other side; there is a little *gariotte* (ancient stone refuge) hidden in the trees. The track is bordered by crumbling stone walls as you go up and cross a field (there is a yellow splash on a walnut tree in the field). The path enters woodland and then goes down a grassy lane past a farm over on the right to reach the D704 crossed earlier (3hrs 45 mins).

16 Cross the road and take a stony track to the left of a garage (Garage Perez) past a field of abandoned old cars and through chestnut trees to reach signposts.
    Turn left, signposted No.4 (you can go straight on here, which is an alternative way back). The track becomes sandy and seems to gain height again. On the right is a plantation of pines and newly planted oak trees (you can hear the road up on the left). Keep bearing round to the right (do not go straight on, or you meet the road before you need to). After a few minutes you reach a T-junction by a wooden cabin where you go down right to reach the D61 road (4hrs).

17 At the road go straight (there is a wooden post with a yellow splash in the field on the other side) across a large open field towards the village cemetery you can see ahead to reach the road and the cemetery wall (4hrs 5 mins).
    Turn down right into the attractive renovated village of St-Geniès, initially down a pretty, narrow road with orchre-coloured houses each side bordered by stone troughs of flowers. Cross the D61 again and continue down a street (ignore no entry sign) past a little restaurant to the right to arrive in the main square. Follow the yellow splashes right and then left, appreciating the wonderful old houses and the magnificent turreted château and church alongside. You will notice the 15th-century Cheylard chapel standing on a rise near the entrance to the village. Inside are some lovely frescoes, but alas the church is often shut. Retrace your steps to the parking (4hrs 15 mins).

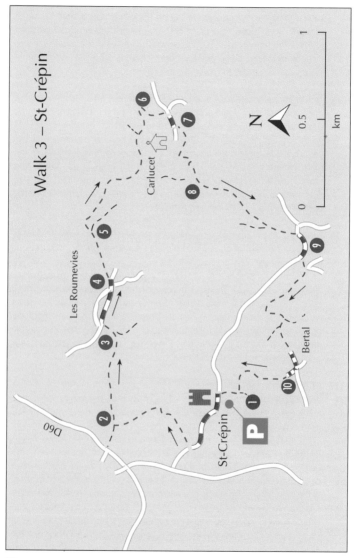

# WALK 3
## St-Crépin and Carlucet:
## A Stroll in the Périgord Noir Countryside

| | |
|---|---|
| **Difficulty:** | Easy walk through undulating countryside |
| **Time:** | 2hrs |
| **Length:** | 6.3km |
| **Map:** | Cartes IGN 2036 ET Top 25 Sarlat/Souillac/Vallée de la Dordogne 1:25,000 |
| **Depart from:** | The parking in front of the church at St-Crépin |
| **Signposting:** | Good – follow well-marked yellow splashes |

A delightful walk between two villages through typical Dordogne scenery of shallow, tree-lined valleys, orchards and fields. With its two parallel towers, the 16th-century Manor de Lacypierre at St-Crépin is charmingly situated in a wooded dip, and is so perfect an example of a small French château that it has been used as a film site and painted many times. It is now in private hands and has been tastefully restored – go into the entrance and you will see a display of how this restoration was done. The 11th-century Romanesque church beside it, dedicated to St Anne, is worth visiting as it has a magnificent altarpiece and ancient holy water font.

### How to get there (from Sarlat)
Take the D704, direction Brive-La-Gaillarde, and after 9km turn right on the D60, direction Salignac (Brive). After 4km turn right, direction St-Crépin, on the D56 and then shortly after left, signposted Vieux St-Crépin. Go down past the château and park in the small parking area opposite the church (there is a map showing other walks that can be done from here).

### Directions

1   Walk up the road you came down, passing the cemetery and the beautifully restored château. Turn right by a stone cross (5 mins) on a jeep track past a charmingly restored house on the left and old barn on the right. The track bears down left by an iron cross and left again by La Grangette which

is a *chambres d'hôtes du charme* (bed & breakfast). Continue right, ignoring a track coming in from the left, to reach another bed & breakfast establishment on the left called Les Granges-Hautes (15 mins).

2   Turn right on a wide track at the sign 'Les Granges-Hautes Accueil' by a large house and garden. The wide track goes through walnut orchards and woodland (ignore a path coming in from the right) to reach a T-junction at a narrow paved road (20 mins).

3   Turn down right towards the hamlet of Les Roumevies, passing a large plastic hanger on the right (used in the autumn to dry tobacco). At a small crossroads go straight (do not turn right where there are also yellow splashes). Shortly after, turn left to go through the hamlet which consists of a few buildings, most of them needing renovation, and continue down a narrow road.

4   Go left at a fork on a jeep track to descend into a shallow valley (30 mins). The track crosses the valley between two fields and continues along the other side, passing a track down right leading to a small lake.

5   **Careful** – go up left a few minutes later on a narrow path through woods going along the valley before bending left into another valley. It passes a

Manoir de Lacypierre, St-Crépin

restored *lavoir* wash trough (why there is a washing place in the middle of nowhere is rather a mystery!) and continues down and up along the side of a hill to meet a T-junction (50 mins).

**6** Go right and continue up past a high wall to reach a house and a paved road. Turn right here and go along for about 100m. Over on the left is the village of Carlucet and up right ahead is the church of Ste-Anne de Carlucet (1hr).

**7** **Careful** – Go left down a grassy path just before the entrance to a big house before you get to the church. *It is worth continuing to the church, which is being restored but gives access to the graveyard, where some of the family tombs are in alcoves in the cemetery wall, which is unusual.* The path goes by a stone wall and then through woods down the side of another shallow valley to reach a curious round building which could be an ancient *gariotte* (the local name for a dry-stone shelter). Continue down to the valley bottom by an overgrown wall (well marked with yellow splashes), crossing the valley by a ruined barn and over a stream hidden in the undergrowth to shortly reach a T-junction at a wide jeep track (1hr 10 mins).

**8** Turn left and continue along the bottom of the valley on this wide track. Continue straight when a track comes in from the right to reach a paved road (1hr 20 mins).

**9** Turn right and look for a large notice board up right in a small clearing explaining the archaeological discoveries in 1983 and 1996 of early Merovingien skeletons (the exact place is marked by a wooden cross). The road curls to the right, and shortly after turn left onto a track to cross the narrow valley; then bear right at the edge of woodland on an attractive upward path with views through the trees into the valley right. You reach the hamlet of Bertal, consisting of one large farm and outbuildings (1hr 45 mins).

**10** Before a long, low farm building turn right off the road (very smelly cow barn along here) through fields and into woodland, going alongside another shallow valley to reach a T-junction at the bottom where you can see buildings over on the right. Turn right to reach the church and car park (2hrs).

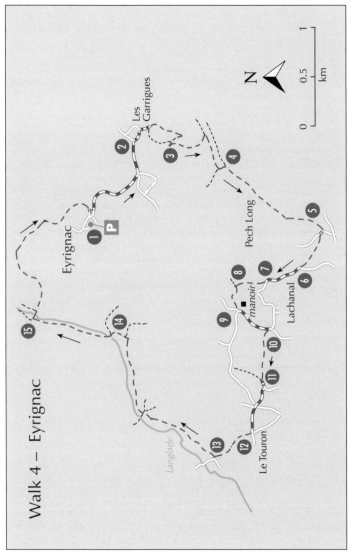

Walk 4 – Eyrignac

# WALK 4
## *Round the Gardens of Eyrignac*

| | |
|---|---|
| **Difficulty:** | An easy, undulating walk with one stiff, short climb |
| **Time:** | 3hrs 15 mins plus around 1 hr to visit the gardens |
| **Length:** | 12.3km |
| **Map:** | Cartes IGN 2036 ET Top 25 Sarlat/Souillac/Vallée de la Dordogne 1:25,000 |
| **Depart from:** | Parking in front of the Eyrignac Gardens |
| **Signposting:** | Excellent – follow yellow splashes but be careful at some of the turnings. Walk no.21 on signposts. |

A delightful walk round the area surrounding the Eyrignac Gardens with lovely open views of the Dordogne countryside. Look out for the masses of enormous lizard orchids on this walk which look spectacular in early June.

### How to get there (from Sarlat)
Take the D47/D56 from Sarlat and follow all indications to the gardens, which are well signposted (13km from Sarlat).

### Directions

1   Go out of the parking, past a cross and walk up the road you came in by (yellow splashes) through an old plantation of tall oak trees. At the road (entrance to the gardens) turn left, direction Salignac, and continue until you come to a narrower road going up to the right, signposted Les Garrigues (15 mins).

2   The road goes up, and at a fork keep right to go through the hamlet, which has an elevated position with glorious, extended views of the rolling Dordogne countryside covered mainly by woodland. At a large, ostentatious house with a high fence to the left, turn down right on a jeep track where there is an old barn (yellow sign on telegraph pole down the path) and a newer one further on. As you start gently down the shoulder of the slope you can appreciate the undulating tree-covered hills extending to

## The Gardens at Eyrignac

Eyrignac is considered to be one of France's most beautiful and original gardens, laid out in the the traditional French style by the Marquis de la Calprenède in the 18th century. Transformed into an English-style garden in the 19th, they were then converted back to their original form by the father of the present owner, Patrick Sermadiras. He painstakingly researched the outlines of the original gardens and, inspired by the Italian 18th-century design, created the Eyrignac gardens as we know them today. It is essentially a leafy landscape, consisting of hornbeams, pines, box and cypresses, many of them sculptured, creating attractive hedges, borders and tree-lined alleys.

Open all year round (guided visits of about one hour):

| | |
|---|---|
| lst January – 31st March | 10.30–12.30 and 14.30 until dusk |
| 1st April – 31st May | 10.00–12.30 and 14.00–19.00 |
| 1st June – 30th September | 9.30–19.00 (open all day) |
| 1st October – 31st December | 10.30–12.30 and 14.30 until dusk |
| Entrance fee: | 7.00 Euro |
| Website: | www.eyrignac.com |

the horizon, where there is a long, low ridge – it is a peaceful pastoral scene very typical of this region of France. Ignore the first track to the left and another right, but after a few minutes take a narrower path to the right. **Careful – this is not easy to see, though there are markings on the fence** (25 mins). You are descending into a tree-covered valley.

3  The path veers left down through juniper bushes and stunted woodland and a few minutes later reaches a T-junction at a jeep track, where you turn down right. The track follows the contour of the hill and turns round the end of the valley, then goes down steeply to reach the bottom. Just before the track reaches a field bear to the right and continue on a wooded path parallel to the valley on the left, reaching another T-junction, where you turn left to cross over grassland to the other side of the valley (40 mins).

4  Turn right and continue along the other side on the edge of the wood on a slightly raised path. The low, tree-covered ridge on the other side of the valley is called the Pech Long, and the narrow stream or watercourse running straight through the fields is called the Mianson, but it is often dried

up. Do not deviate from the delightfully flat, leafy path until you reach a road (1hr).

5 Turn right for a few metres and then turn off the road left on a wide track. Shortly after, look for a fork and go right (well marked with yellow splashes), signposted Lachanal/La Tour. The grassy track goes up steeply away from the valley and reaches houses and fields at a narrow road, where there is a large wooden barn and a modern house left (1hr 10 mins).

6 Go right past another wooden barn into the hamlet of Lachanal, which appears to have a micro-climate – persimmon, mulberry and fig trees trees with tubs of canna lilies give the hamlet an exotic air! There is also a lovely view to the right, as you are in open upland country.

7 Continue down the road past a field of kiwi bushes and a small vineyard. Where it bends to the left go straight on a grassy track, where you can see a beautiful manor house up on the left.

8 You reach a T-junction at a jeep track (more kiwi bushes up here), where you turn left past a very nice renovated house (La Borie de la Tour) with a *chambres d'hôtes* sign (*lovely cosmos flowers in the garden*). It looks an inviting place to stay and has a lovely view. The road curls round the top

*Sculptured hedges – the Gardens of Eyrignac*

*Evening light on hornbeam hedges – the Gardens of Eyrignac*

of a grassy depression through walnut orchards, fig trees and more kiwi plantations to reach a crossroads (1hr 25 mins).

**9**   Turn down left past the manor house and gardens – there is a sign saying 'Entrée Manoir de Latour 14th–16th-century Monument Historique' (these historical houses are only open a few days a year as they are privately owned) – there are glorious extended views as you go down this road.

**10**   Shortly after the manor and before you get to a crossroads by an ugly house, look for a yellow splash indicating to go sharp right (**not easy to see**). This is an undulating track over fields – keep straight and ignore any other tracks coming in. It descends to another road at a corner, where you turn right round another shallow valley towards the hamlet of Le Touron (left goes to la Veyssière) (1hr 40 mins).

**11**   Go straight at the next crossroads and continue towards Le Touron. Just before you reach the hamlet up left, go straight down a jeep track towards an intersection.

**12**   **Careful** – just before the track reaches the intersection where there is a sign to Manoir d'Eyrignac, go right on a grassy track (yellow arrow on tree). At the intersection another walk comes in and goes up to the hamlet; this could be confusing, as there are other yellow splashes here (1hr 50 mins).

The track goes through fields and then descends into woodland. Stick to the main track to reach the bottom of a wide, shallow valley called Langlade, which is also the name of the narrow watercourse running through the fields.

13  Turn right and walk for 2.5km along the side of this delightful valley, which has large fields bordered by woods. It becomes wooded, narrowing slightly, and just after you notice an enormous field behind you the track reaches a jeep track (2hrs 20 mins).

14  Turn down left at the Moulin de Coulaud on the map (couldn't see a mill anywhere!) and cross the Langlade watercourse to the other side of the valley. The track continues past a high eroded bank to the left, and afterwards there are lines of high poplars to the right (2hrs 45 mins).

15  **Be careful** – at the trees turn right (sign long way before) on a wide track which goes through the poplar trees and by a big eroded rock on the left. The track continues through mixed deciduous woodland (oak, beech, hornbeam, sycamore) going steadily upward and then out of the woods at a small walnut orchard. Ahead is the green slope of a high hill, which you circle round to the right and continue along the bottom of the slope. Then go gently up at the end to reach the buildings and beautifully sculptured evergreen bushes of the Eyrignac Gardens to reach the car park (3hrs 15 mins).

*The Gardens of Eyrignac*

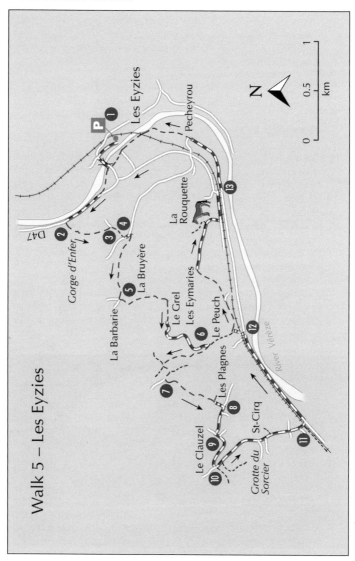

Walk 5 – Les Eyzies

# WALK 5
## *Les Eyzies on the Vézère River*

| | |
|---|---|
| **Difficulty:** | Easy, undulating walk |
| **Time:** | 3hrs 30 mins plus 10 mins to see Grotte de Cirq. Also leave time to visit the National Museum of Prehistory in Les Eyzies. |
| **Length:** | 11.9km |
| **Map:** | Cartes IGN1936 ET Top 25 Les Eyzies/Vallées de la Dordogne et de la Vézère 1:25,000 |
| **Depart from:** | Parking de la Vézère (free municipal parking) by the river |
| **Signposting:** | Rather confusing – well-indicated red/white splashes of the GR6 plus yellow splashes, but they come and go. Follow walk directions carefully. Note: sometimes the markings are at least 100m before the actual turning. |

An easy walk with some lovely views of the cliffs and grottos above the Vézère river. It can be combined with a visit to the National Museum of Prehistory (Musée Nationale de la Préhistoire) or one of the many grottos in the area. The museum is open all year round, 9.30–12.00 and 14.00–18.00. Free entrance every first Sunday in the month. It takes about an hour to visit. See walk no.6 and 'A short history of the Dordogne' (Introduction) for further information about Les Eyzies and the Vézère valley.

### How to get there (from Sarlat)
Take the D6 from Sarlat signposted Les Eyzies/Périgeux, which after 2km changes to the D47. Continue for 19km to the outskirts of Les Eyzies. Follow signs 'centre ville' and go down the main street. At the end turn left at a signpost 'Parking de la Vézère', which is a free municipal parking area by the river.

### Directions

1   Go out of the parking (there is a large map here of the area) and turn right on the road. Walk along past houses, patches of bamboo and a canoeing rental service before turning left on the bridge across the Vézère river on

Poppy fields near Les Eyzies

a special undulating walkway for walkers, where there is a good view down the river. At the end of the bridge at a red/white GR cross, go obliquely left on a gravel path that goes down and under the bridge (you will see a red/white GR splash on the wooden fence). The path goes along the side of the river and then goes up by the side of the D47. You pass a staircase cut in the rock face on the other side of the road, which is the entrance to the Speleology (potholing) Museum (20 mins).

2   **Careful** – turn left shortly afterwards on a pedestrian crossing (yellow mark on a tree on the other side) into the Gorge d'Enfer ('hell gorge'). This is a dank, dark gorge with a high fence and a stream on the right, with over-hanging high cliffs, left, where there are man-made holes in the rock face. *You can imagine prehistoric man taking refuge here and making the holes to support wooden beams for his shelter.* At the start of the gorge, over on the right, is the Abri de Poisson (a grotto with the fossil of a fish). It can be visited on request only in July and August. The gorge continues upwards fairly steeply along a jeep track with a sinister woodland area on the right to reach the top at a large open field (30 mins).

3   Follow the path, right, where there is an impressive gate and a modern wall, left, which appears to be the entrance to pastureland and nothing more. As you go along the track you can see the hamlet of Le Bil up to the right. After a few minutes you reach a road.

4   Turn left and then shortly after, where the road starts to round a corner, turn down hard right following a GR splash and wooden yellow sign (35

mins). *This track was taken by the* anciennes carrières de kaolin *(carts carrying clay from the quarries), and you can see the marks of the cartwheels on the rocks.* The track goes up through oak and chestnut trees (ignore any paths coming in) to reach crossroads by some overhead telephone wires, opposite a house called La Barbarie (50 mins).

5   Turn left on the road past a large house called Le Bruyère. At another house, right, continue straight on a jeep track (do not go down right before the house) and ignore GR cross. Following yellow splashes continue through woods to emerge shortly after at an attractive area of fields and a large farm called Le Grel, left. Continue on (ignore track to the right at an entrance to the farm) to reach a paved road (main entrance to the farm) and bear right. Wind down through woods towards a shallow valley which appears on the right.

6   **Careful** – on the way down look for a wide turn-off bending sharp right – this is confusing, as there are pink splashes but no red/white GR or yellow splashes and it is easy to miss (1hr 10 mins). **For a much shorter walk continue down the road and turn left at the bottom onto a jeep track where there are yellow splashes – see no.12 below.** Keep to the wide, flat track along the side of the valley where there are fields and poplar trees. The track bears left and crosses the valley and the narrow watercourse running through it to enter woods on the other side (1hr 20 mins).

7   Turn right and go along the other side of the valley for a few minutes and then look for a GR6 sign indicating a sharp turning up to the left on a narrower track up the side of the hill. You arrive at a small, open plateau where you can see the hamlet of Les Plagnes just ahead. Make your way across the fields by the occasional walnut tree to reach a small T-junction, where you turn left and walk by some houses (1hr 35 mins).

8   Turn right again shortly after at a further T-junction, passing a huge long barn and open green fields. You come to another farm on the right with a *pigonnier* (dovecot). Continue down, ignoring a road left to Bimbonnerie and a path with a pink arrow.

9   Shortly afterwards turn down left (the hamlet of Le Clauzel is up right). The road curls round to the right to meet a larger road at a charming iron cross on a stone plinth (1hr 50 mins).

**10 Careful** – at the turning, do not turn up to the right where there are yellow
splashes or take the track up beside the iron cross, but turn left and walk
down the road towards St-Cirq (1hr 50 mins).

As you walk through the village you get a good view ahead of the
wide Vézère river valley with a church over on the right. Go straight down
over a small crossroads by a charming stream, ignoring a track to the right
to reach the railway and a small level crossing. Just afterwards you meet a
road again (2hrs 5 mins).

### Detour to Grotte du Sorcier

As you walk down the road the GR6 goes off to the right, signposted Grotte
de Cirq (also called Grotte du Sorcier). It is worth making a detour to look
at the grotto, which is in a quaint setting by a little house built into the rock
with a pigeonnier above. Opposite is a large clump of bamboo. A visit to
the grotto costs 4 euros (not seen by author). The detour takes about 10 mins,
which does not include a visit to the grotto.

**11** Turn left following the sign 'Les Eyzies 4km' and go down the road with
the railway line left. There are fields between the road and the river, but at
one stage the road is very near the riverbank.

**12 Careful** – look for a turning to the left which goes underneath the railway
where there are two large red and white posts, signposted Le Grel, La
Bruyère and La Mouthe (2hrs 20 mins). Shortly after go right at a T-junction and then do a hairpin right onto a jeep track, where yellow splashes
start again. This track goes along the front of a low, tree-covered hill to
reach a charming lost conglomeration of ancient houses called Le Peuch,
which are partially set into the rocky cliffs behind.

Before you get to a level crossing, turn to the left by a laurel hedge on
a path passing a gate standing on its own and leading to nothing! The track
goes through woodland, but on the right is a huge green field that seems
to go on for ever! You pass a *gîte d'étape* at Les Eymaries and continue on,
with the woods on the left and the lovely field on the right, passing caves
in the rocky cliffs. As you turn the corner to cross the end of the field there
is a riding school on the left with a number of horses in the paddocks. The
road bears to the left; do not go through the railway tunnel straight on, but
continue to reach a T-junction (2hrs 50 mins).

**13** Go right over a level crossing and then bear left on the Chemin de Pecheyrou, signposted La Tuilière/Le Pecheyrou. Continue along on a flat path going through wide-open fields and vineyards through the hamlet of Pecheyrou, with the railway behind it and, further behind, the bigger hamlet of La Rouquette.

*In spring the fields are a mass of red poppies, a striking contrast to the dark holes of caves in the high cliffs above the river which can be seen on the skyline.* The track bends to the left towards Les Eyzies through fields of crops, as does the river on the right, though you cannot see it until you reach the outskirts of the village. You near the riverbank as you bear left and go under the railway bridge to continue along near the river. The parking area is visible on the other side, but in order to reach it you have to walk straight and up a gravel track to cross the bridge, then turn right back to the parking (3hrs 30 mins).

*Grotte de Cirq near Les Eyzies*

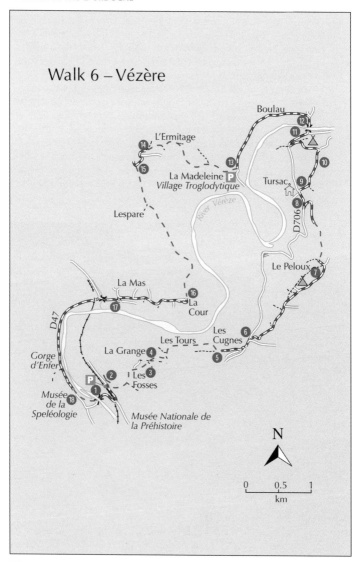

Walk 6 – Vézère

# WALK 6
## *Les Gorges de la Vézère*

| | |
|---|---|
| **Difficulty:** | Medium because of its length – otherwise easy |
| **Time:** | 5hrs plus 45 mins if you visit La Madeleine Troglodyte village |
| **Length:** | 18.2km |
| **Map:** | Cartes IGN 1936 ET Top 25 Les Eyzies/Vallées de la Dordogne et de la Vézère 1:25,000 |
| **Depart from:** | Parking in front of the train station at Les Eyzies-de-Tayac |
| **Signposting:** | Good – follow the red/white splashes of the GR36 and then yellow splashes (walk no.8) |

Although this is a long walk, it is an easy one, as you go over undulating coun-tryside, through extensive woodland, open fields and shallow valleys. There are extended views, and the cliffs along the meandering River Vézère are often on the horizon. There is the added attraction of a visit to the fascinating troglodyte village of La Madeleine halfway round the walk.

The unpretentious village of Les Eyzies-de-Tayac nestles under overhanging cliffs, one of which is crowned with an ugly statue of a caveman. Situated at the confluence of the Vézère and Beune rivers, its claim to fame is that the earliest traces of prehistoric man have been found in the surrounding cliffs. In caves and overhangs, caused by erosion of limestone in the rocky cliffs of the river, early man installed himself and left behind innumerable relics of his passage. The area has become a pilgrimage for thousands of tourists, but curiously the village has remained unsophisticated. It houses the National Museum of Prehistory, which is worth a visit. (See 'A short history of the Dordogne' (Introduction) and walk no.5 for further information.)

The 12th-century church of Les Eyzies de Tayac-Sireil (on the St-Jacques de Compostella trail) is 5 mins from the station where the walk starts, but can only be visited on demand.

### How to get there (from Sarlat)
Take the D6 out of Sarlat, signposted Les Eyzies, which after 2km changes to the D47. On the outskirts of the village turn left on the D706 and follow sign 'Centre

Ville'. Drive down the main street, and at a corner just before the road goes over the Vézère river you will see a sign straight on indicating SNCF Gare (railway station). Drive on this narrower road for a few hundred metres and park in front of the small railway station (21km from Sarlat).

## Directions

1    Facing the station turn left and walk back along the road for a few minutes. Just before the road you came in by and a 'Stop' sign, take a sharp turning up left. The red/white splashes of the GR36 are on a tree further on, but not visible from the road. Walk by houses on a narrow lane. As you turn a corner you will see a large overhanging rock to the right with a plaque in it stating that in 1868 the bones of a man dating from the Aurignacienne age (30,000 years ago) were discovered at this site when they were building the railway station. Continue upwards on a stony track (5 mins).

2    Ignore a path coming in from the left as you go round a hairpin bend and walk on as the track narrows, wending its way uphill before flattening out. Go left at a fork by a field joining a wider track and walk round the top of the field to arrive at a few houses called Les Fosses (20 mins). At an intersection by a renovated house to the right go straight to reach the top of a field with the garden of the house to the right (20 mins).

3    Go left on a track, appreciating the extended views to the left, including the cliffs bordering the Vézère river, as you walk along and into chestnut woods.

4    Continue straight at a small crossroads and a few minutes later bear left at a fork (cross on tree to right). The track now undulates round the contour of the hill (Les Tours on the map) through oak and then deciduous wood as it starts to descend. **Careful** – keep on the main path in the wood following the red/white GR splashes here and ignore the path with yellow splashes going off left. The woods thin out and you pass a ruined building before coming to a T-junction.

5    Turn left, and shortly afterwards the track becomes paved at a house, right, called Les Sables. Walk down the road, which is part of a new development of attractive 'up market' houses being built here, to reach a wider road (D706) at Les Cugnes. Turn left and, ignoring a road coming in from the right, continue along for a few minutes (50 mins).

**6**   Turn up right, signposted La Ferme de Peloux (the GR splash is hidden behind the signpost). This is a smart paved road going up for quite a way through prestigious large houses, some newly built, but all with lots of land and beautiful gardens. At the top you pass oak and pine woods (do not go up left into the pine woods) to reach a high-class camping site on the left called Le Peloux, where the road narrows. Continue on by fields, left, and woods, right, to reach a crossroads (1hr 25 mins).

**7**   Turn left and go straight (do not take the immediate track to the left), and shortly after turn right at an intersection. Keep on the main track, descending a hill through young woodland. Look out for a dilapidated stone water source hidden in the brambles, right, that you can hear gurgling away. Further down the track becomes paved (house up on the right called La Peyrier) and comes out of the woodland, where you get a wonderful view left over the river, the village of Tursac and the Marzac château, with its many towers, perched atop a wooded hill on the other side of the Vézère valley. Keep on the road wending down. **Careful** – turn sharp right off the road (splashes) just before a white house and then left just before the entrance to another house. This path is really just cutting off a corner passing an old washhouse to reach the D706 (1hr 45 mins).

**8**   Turn right and walk into the village of Tursac. *There is a fortified church here with a square Romanesque tower as this area used to be the frontier between the Duchy of Aquitaine and France – it has an unusual interior with a series of cupolas. Unfortunately you cannot visit churches in France easily as they are usually locked.*

**9**   Take the turning, right, opposite the church, going up out of the village and passing a delightful little restaurant (La Source) on the right. Keep to the paved road, where again there are extended views and you can clearly see the line of cliffs the other side of the valley.

**10**   Turn down left by a broken stone cross to the right past a prestigious three-star camping site on the right to meet the D706 road again (2hrs 10 mins). **This is really a diversion to avoid the road going straight through Tursac, which is difficult to walk along**.

**11**   Cross over the road and go right on a narrow grassy verge (no defined path here), past a big *auberge* called La Peche Lune and down the hill, turning to the left at the bottom across the River Vézère. The river here is attractively wide and flows strongly through lush green fields, its banks bordered by trees. Cross the river and walk along a short stretch of raised road lined with Schumacher trees and fields beyond. At the end turn left following a sign 'Village Troglodytique médiéval'. **You have left the GR36 at this turning and from now to the end of the walk follow yellow splashes** (2hrs 20 mins).

## Detour

The troglodyte village is worth visiting, so continue down the road past an interesting map showing all the prehistoric sites in the area to reach the entrance building. Calculate around 45 mins for the visit.

This is an exceptional natural site that has attracted man since prehistoric times. Beneath a rock shelter on the banks of the River Vézère this Palaeolithic site has given its name to a whole cultural epoch – the Magdalenian (12,000–8000BC). Halfway up the cliff face can be found converted cave dwellings, probably inhabited from the Middle Ages until the beginning of the 20th century. There are also remnants of a 15th-century château, chapel and lookout posts.

*Grotte de la Madeleine near Les Eyzies*

**12** Keep on the flat road bordering this delightful valley with its wide green fields, left, and the river running through, passing the hamlet of Boulau. After a while there is quite a long haul up a hill through woods to reach the entrance to La Madeleine (troglodyte village) at a car park. **Careful** – just before the car park take a narrow track off right marked with yellow splashes (2hrs 40 mins).

**13** Go back to the track before the car park and walk up this stony mule path passing a large field, right, with a derelict house (why has nobody snapped it up?). The track is gradually descending into a shallow valley. Some 10 mins later continue round a corner on the main track when a path comes in from the right. The path descends to reach the boggy, tree-covered area at the bottom of the valley. At a T-junction bear right (yellow cross left) to cross the valley over a water channel. Continue upwards on a sunken track through boxwood flanked by dark, dank sinister trees, many covered in moss and ivy, their branches extending over the track so that you feel you are walking through a high tunnel. At a T-junction deep in the woods where there is a mossy stone wall in front, turn right, and soon afterwards the dense woods thin out. Go along the side of a hill, bearing left across open pasture and then uphill on the other side of the valley. Keep on the main track, ignoring a track coming in from the left, to continue up, with a field down on the right, to reach another T-junction at a paved road.

**14** Go left (down right is the private entrance to a house called L'Ermitage) up a steep hill, ignoring a road coming in from the left, to reach a house, right, and a vineyard, left, where the road curls round to the right (3hrs 30 mins).

**15** Turn left off the road signposted Ferme Lespare. **(You can go right here as there is an alternative but longer route down to the river valley.)** Walk along the side of the vineyard, going into woodland where there is a tall radio antenna and through attractive open fields; you are on the highest point of the walk (all of 209m) and there are extended views in all directions. Bear left when you reach the entrance to La Ferme Lespare (yellow splashes) and head into chestnut wood. Keep on the main path bearing left a few minutes later where there are two gated fields and continue through scattered woodland consisting of deciduous trees, pines and bushy undergrowth, mainly bracken. The track starts to descend and there are lovely open views to the right, past a hunter's look-out post in a tree, right – *when we passed the hunters were installed there with their guns, so we hoped we were not going to be shot at!* As you continue descending you can see

83

the wide openings of caves in the cliffs on the other side of river. The track passes a large cowshed and then reaches the large farm of La Cour, where there are a number of big barns with tobacco hanging to dry in long rows; the smell of tobacco is overwhelming (3hrs 55 mins).

**16** The road curves around La Cour farm and outbuildings and continues down through green fields to a T-junction. Turn left (right goes up to the farm) and continue down, going right at a further junction (the road left is a dead end to Les Guignes farm). The river is over on the left beyond cultivated fields and there is a tall ivy-covered bank on the right. Ignore two roads coming down from the right; the second one, signposted Le Mas, is the alternative walk route joining up. You can see a large red bridge spanning the river ahead, which you think you are going to cross, but this is the railway. Instead the road crosses a narrow stream on an old concrete bridge to reach the busy D47 (4hrs 25 mins).

**17** Turn left – this is initially not a pleasant road to walk along and be careful when you go under the railway bridge. However, the grassy verge on the left becomes wider as you pass the amazing caves and buildings built into the side of the rock face the other side of the road. You see the Abri Prehistorique de Laugerie Haute (one of the largest rock shelters in the area, inhabited 24,000 to 14,000BC), the Laugerie Basse (inhabited 14,000BC to the present day) and the natural grotto of Grand Roc (open for visits, large parking on the left).

You are now walking above the river with the cliffs towering above you the other side of the road. There is a little wall between you and the road, making walking more pleasant as you see Les Eyzies come into view. On the other side is the entrance to the Gorge d'Enfer (walk no.5) and the Speleological Museum – another place worth visiting if you like burrowing in dark places! **The GR6 has joined from the gorge, so red/white splashes will appear again**.

**18** Soon after turn left onto a grassy path along the side of the river and away from the road. Go under the road bridge (GR splashes) and double back right to go up a slope and right again on an undulating footpath over the bridge. Cross the road on a pedestrian crossing (be careful – the cars go fast round here) in front of a hotel. The back of the railway station is straight ahead, so cross the tracks (do watch for trains!) and go through the station to the parking, or alternatively go round by the road (5hrs).

# WALK 7
## *Around the Château of Les Milandes*

| | |
|---|---|
| **Difficulty:** | Easy, open, undulating walk with one short, steep stretch towards the end |
| **Time:** | 3hrs 45 mins plus around 1hr to look round the château |
| **Length:** | 13.4km |
| **Maps:** | Cartes IGN 1936 ET Top 25 Les Eyzies/Vallées de la Dordogne et de la Vézère and Cartes IGN Série Bleu 2037 Ouest Domme 1:25,000 |
| **Depart from:** | Parking near the château |
| **Signposting:** | Good, but follow yellow splashes carefully as they are not always easy to see. On one short stretch there are no splashes |

This walk is particularly pleasant, as much of the way is through high, open fields with extensive views in all directions, particularly of the fairy-tale turrets of the château of Les Milandes, probably the most attractive of all the Dordogne châteaux. This walk entails a high number of road crossings and constant turnings to right and left, but it is extremely well signposted and it would be hard to go wrong.

The Château des Milandes owes its celebrity to two women, namely Claude de Cardaillac and Josephine Baker. It was originally constructed in 1489 by François de Caumont to please his ambitious young wife, Claude, who wanted a magnificent châteaux in the flamboyant Italian style popular at that time. She achieved her dream, as it is a real 'fairy-tale' castle of ornamental towers, gargoyles and ornate windows set high on a hill for all to admire! It remained in the same family until the Revolution.

In 1937, the famous American cabaret artist Josephine Baker fell in love with Les Milandes, finally buying it in 1946 where her marriage to Jo Bouillon took place in the château chapel. Making extensive renovations, she turned it into the house of her dreams and created a home for her many adopted children. Unfortunately she fell on hard times and the place was sold in 1969. It is now a museum to her memory and shows her life and the famous people she hobnobbed with – there is also a fascinating display of her flamboyant clothes, jewellery and her luxurious bathroom.

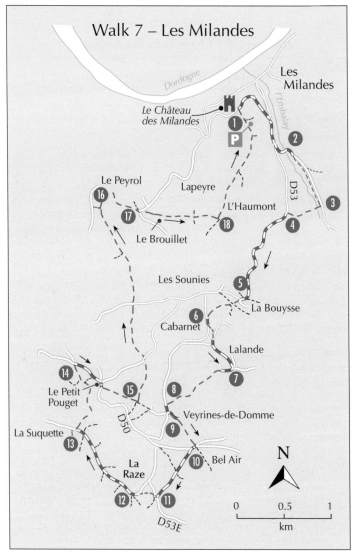

# Walk 7 – Les Milandes

Château open April–September 10.00–18.00. July–August 9.30–19.30. October 10.00–12.00 and 14.00–17.00. Closed November to March. Near the château is also a Bird of Prey Museum where falconry is demonstrated.

**How to get there (from Sarlat)**
Take the D57 signposted Bergerac and then turn onto the D703, signposted Château les Milandes 8km. After 2km turn back onto the D57, which crosses the Dordogne, and then turn right on the D53 following all signs to the château. There is a sharp right-hand turn off the D53 which takes you up up through the hamlet of Les Milandes and past the château itself. Turn left where parking is indicated (18.4km from Sarlat).

**Directions**

1  Go out of the car park and turn right on the road you came in by. Walk past the château and down the hill through the hamlet of Les Milandes to reach the D53 and turn right, direction Veyrines and Belves (10 mins).

2  Walk along the road for a few minutes and take a narrower road to the left (yellow splashes) which goes down to a shallow valley where there are walnut trees and fields of maize. At the bottom cross over a stream (Ruisseau L'Embalay), left, and continue round on the opposite side of the valley. Look for a yellow splash indicating right on a path going parallel to the road, which soon reaches a fork (25 mins).

3  Take the right fork (the left one also has yellow splashes but is a longer way round). The path crosses the valley and goes over the stream again, bearing round to the right then left uphill beside a field with a wood to the right. The bushy path becomes steeper as it goes up through a tunnel of boxwood with a wall one side and reaches the D53 road again at a place called L'Haumont (one big house). *When we were walking in October we saw the most incredible display of wild cyclamen flowering on the bank and beyond the hedge under some trees* (35 mins).

4  Turn left and continue up the road. As you get higher there are extensive views of the surrounding countryside including the Château des Milandes and the Château Marqueyssac to the right. You can see the cliffs of the Dordogne river valley but not the river itself. There is a magnificent slope of green down to the right bordered by poplar trees with a huge field of maize alongside as the road bends right and then left to reach a couple of houses and a funeral directors, part of the hamlet of La Bouysse.

*Château des Milandes*

5    Just beyond here (avoid first track to left) and at the end of a laurel hedge
     turn down left and then almost immediately right on a stony jeep track (50
     mins). The track goes down into a sort of dip (ignore any tracks coming in)
     and goes up again to reach a large house at a place called Cabarnet.

6    Turn left past a stagnant expanse of water, which goes under the road to
     flow by the house – it could be an old mill. **Careful** – as the road reaches
     a long barn right, go down left (no visible yellow splashes) on a path to
     reach another narrow road (1hr 5 mins). Go up right for a few metres to
     meet a slightly wider road, where you turn left towards a nice house on
     the left called Lalande and a small crossroads.

7    Turn right (yellow splashes not easy to see) and pass in front of an unat-
     tractive low bungalow (looks as if you are going through the front garden!).
     The path has done a large curve and you can see Lalande down on the
     right as you climb higher on a wide lane. At the top walk along a wide
     bank with a walnut orchard right. On a bend just before a barn look for
     yellow splashes indicating right and then immediately left. The track
     descends to a road where there are long plastic tunnels for drying tobacco.
     *The tobacco is dried by placing a long tube pierced with holes down the*
     *centre of the tunnel, which blows hot air out over the hanging leaves*
     (1hr 26 mins).

8    Go left up the road to the attractive hamlet of Veyrines-de-Domme at a
     junction with the old church facing you. **Careful here – ignore yellow**

**splashes going to the right as you are doing a shortcut.** For the next short part of the walk there are no yellow splashes. Go left through the village square where there is a very elaborate, tall maypole in front of the *mairie* (see 'The Périgord Noir' (Introduction) for an explanation) and past a school called Ecole Hampshire. *This is a summer school for English children who are sent out from a private school in England to learn the language – what a good idea* (1hr 30 mins)!

9 **Careful** (no splashes) – take a narrow, grassy path on the left-hand side of the school which gives you a good view of the old buildings of this small establishment. The path goes upwards to reach a junction at a place called Bel Air.

10 Turn right on the D50, and a few minutes later go off left on a narrow paved road following a sign indicating Truc Haut (yellow splashes again), passing a house on the right. Keep on the road, where there are lovely extended views in all directions, passing an attractive renovated house on the right to reach the D53E (1hr 45 mins).

11 Turn right (do not go straight across the road on a jeep track) and continue for a few metres before going left on a grassy track through a field and small chestnut wood to come to yet another road.

12 Go left on the road, which bends right to reach the pretty hamlet of La Raze. You are on high ground going along a wide ridge where the views on all sides are extensive. The road goes down the shoulder of the ridge and carries on past tobacco tunnels.

13 **Careful here as the yellow splash is not easy to see** – just after the tunnels and before the garden of a private house (at a place called La Suquette on the map) turn down right (2hrs). This is another leafy lane descending into a small dip and around a field by the side of a wood before winding uphill. Keep to the main path all the way and at a fork go left (cross on tree right). The path goes out into lovely open, wide fields, again planted with tobacco, and then bends gently upwards to reach a road at the top (2hrs 15 mins).

14 Go right on the road to arrive at an intersection at Le Petit Pouget. Go right on the D50 (do not go left on the D53 indicating Château des Milandes) continuing for a few metres before bearing up left behind a red-brick building. The path goes up through some tall pines and chestnuts, past a

new house on the left where it becomes a wide jeep track. Continue straight, ignoring any tracks coming in, through woodland to an intersection near a *pigonnier*. **You have now almost done a circle from the village of Veyrines-de-Domme, which is now straight ahead. A track with yellow splashes joins from the right and there are a number of yellow signposts** (2hrs 30 mins).

**15** Go left following sign Les Milandes and keep straight. Soon the extensive views disappear as the path goes into stunted woodland, descending the shoulder and out of the wood again to the road at a hamlet called Le Pouget on the left. Go straight across the road onto a grassy track which goes gently up again and then down by the side of a wood, becoming bushy and passing a walnut orchard before reaching another road. Cross the road and go straight along a fairly flat track through woodland for about 10 mins before you branch down to the right (clearly marked on a telephone pole). Still in woods, the old mule track becomes irritatingly stony as it descends into a woody depression, passing a house to the left to reach a stream by a huddle of houses called Le Peyrol at the bottom – an idyllic spot in the middle of nowhere! Here the GR64 joins from over the bridge (3hrs).

**16** **Careful here** – before crossing the stream and meeting the road turn right along a grassy path (markings on a tree not immediately obvious). The narrow stony path climbs up the hill steeply through woodland for about 10 mins to arrive at the top by a road. There is an *auberge* here called Le Brouillet and a large camping area (3hrs 15 mins).

**17** Go right on the road for a few metres, then left and right again (after the *auberge,* not before) opposite the camping site of Les Pastourels. The path (signposted 'Pays Josephine Baker' passes the *accueil* (reception) of Le Brouillet and becomes fenced for a while as it traverses wide green fields with extensive views each side and the beautiful turrets of the Château des Milandes over on the left. The path passes a little stone shelter *gariotte,* left, and starts to descend. Shortly afterwards there is a sign left indicating 'fontaine and lavoir' of Lapeyre. **This is a diversion to the fountain and washing trough of Lapeyre which can be taken if desired** (3hrs 25 mins).

**18** The track goes through delightful open fields and turns left at a T-junction. There is a wooded escarpment on the right as the track descends round a hill and continues to the parking area of the château (3hrs 45 mins).

# WALK 8
## *Le Chemin de Cazenac: Walk around Beynac*

| | |
|---|---|
| **Difficulty:** | Medium – up and down but never for too long |
| **Time:** | 3hrs plus time to explore the village and visit the château |
| **Length:** | 11.2km |
| **Map:** | Cartes IGN 1936 ET Top 25 Les Eyzies/Vallées de la Dordogne et de la Vézère 1:25,000 |
| **Depart from:** | Parking Le Crouzet – Beynac |
| **Signposting:** | Good – follow yellow splashes and some signs walk no.7 until Cazenac, when the route in this guide follows a more direct way back |

From this walk you have a magnificent view of four well-known Dordogne châteaux as well as the river, and as it is not long or difficult there is plenty of time to visit the village and château of Beynac at the end.

With the château perched on a cliff top, and the houses below crushed between the rocks and the riverbank, Beynac is one of the most spectacular villages in France. The origins of the castle are obscure, but it was probably built as a fortress in the eighth century. During the Hundred Years' War it fell into the hands of the English and in 1195 Richard the Lionheart gave it as a fief to one of his favourite captains called Mercadier. It was attacked and partially destroyed in 1214 by Simon de Montfort, to be rebuilt in its present form by the Seigneur de Beynac. Beynac was the seat of one on the four baronies of Périgord. In the last few years it has gone through extensive restoration and reconstruction.

The castle can be visited every day 10.00–12.00 and 14.00–18.30. There is a guided tour that takes about an hour.

### How to get there (from Sarlat)
From the centre of Sarlat follow signs to Bergerac/Cahors. At the first roundabout turn right, direction Bergerac/Beynac. From then on follow all signs to Beynac even though the numbers of the roads change from D46 to D57 and D49 to D703. As you enter the village continue until you see a sign up right indicating 'Parking Le Crouzet', which is a free parking area on the way to the château (12km from Sarlat).

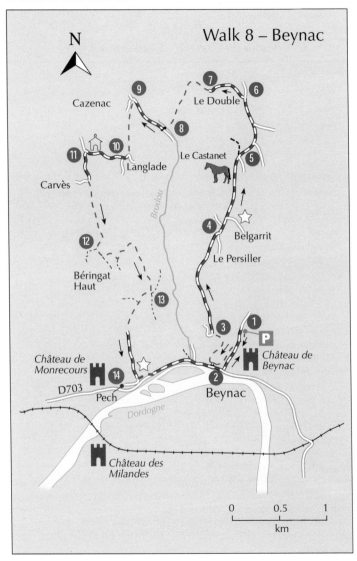

## Directions

1   Go behind the parking onto a raised path and turn right (yellow splash on tree). The path runs parallel to the road and reaches a small wooden building with a thatched roof called a *hutte gauloise* (*looks like a drawing from an Asterix book!*). Cross the road and go down left for a few metres past another parking area and then turn up right. Keep to the upper path, following the yellow splashes, down to the village of Beynac, looking over the ancient tiled roofs of an enchanting cluster of houses, dominated by the castle, with the Dordogne river and valley below. The four châteaux of Marqueyssac, Castelnaud, Fayrac and Lacoste are also visible on the horizon.

2   Turn up right by an old renovated building, following the yellow arrow number 7, towards an iron cross. Soon afterwards the road becomes a track, bearing right and upwards out of the village, with an old brick wall to the right and continuing extended views of the village, Dordogne river and surrounding countryside to the left. The track becomes woody, passing an old house, right, with a nice terrace on the other side of the track, and then a modern house, left, by a corner at a paved road (15 mins).

3   Turn right and continue upwards, ignoring a jeep track on the right marked 'Le Couztal'. Continue through open fields and woods, passing a barn to the left and old house to the right. The track is level (sometimes paved and sometimes not) as it goes along the side of the hill. Keep straight on, passing a large manor house to the right, part of the hamlet of Le Persiller, and then a little *gariotte* (round stone building) just before the road starts to go up again to reach a T-junction (30 mins).

4   Turn left, signposted Le Double/Langlade/7, on a paved road rising gently through more open country. **Detour** – a few minutes later turn right (there is a small arrow 'Pointe de Vue Beynac') for a wonderful view over Beynac and the Dordogne valley; do not continue down to the village of Belgarrit (below) but take photos and admire the view before retracing your steps (takes about 5 mins). Turn right and continue along the top of the hill, past occasional buildings to reach a riding establishment and fields of horses (Le Castanet on the map).

5   Immediately after Le Castanet the road bends right to meet a wider road at a T-junction, where you keep left, signposted 'Le Double'/walk no.7.

Keep on the main road, ignoring a track to the right. Turn left at the next road junction and continue for about 300m to another junction.

**6** Branch left here by some houses towards Le Double (straight on is St-André) and round a wide turn where green slopes sweep down on the left to meet woodland in a wide, shallow valley with lovely views. Soon you reach the hamlet of Le Double (1hr).

**7** Go through the houses but do not turn right where the yellow splash seems to indicate, instead go on a few metres till the paved road stops in front of the entrance to a house and then turn right. The narrow paved road becomes a jeep track after a new house, turns left and descends into a beech wood, continuing down into a shallow, tree-covered valley called Vallée de Brudou. There are occasional attractive clearings to the right as the path goes into the bottom of the valley through woods covered in ivy.

**8** **Careful** – where there is a large yellow cross in front, turn right to cross the narrow valley bottom. Leave the woodland to walk along the side of a field on the left and over a watercourse (this runs through the valley) to reach another paved road where you turn right and continue to the next junction (1hr 20 mins).

**9** **Careful here** – where the road turns to the left signposted 'Cazenac, Pech Viel, Les Garrigues' take a narrow path just before the turning which has yellow splashes. Clamber up the bank – the path climbs up through low trees and tall pines, through two attractive fields (*some interesting flowers here including the tongue orchid*) and becomes a narrow lane before arriving at the top of the *pech* (low summit) by the garage entrance of a newly built house. Turn left and soon the track becomes paved as you enter the beautifully restored village of Langlade, where there are some attractive houses for rent (1hr 35 mins).

In the tiny centre of the hamlet you have a choice of directions: **straight on to Beringot/Beynac 7km (a shorter way back, not walked by author) or right to Cazenac and its interesting church**.

**10** Turn right towards Cazenac (sign not immediately apparent) on a narrow road (**not** straight ahead on the grassy path) from which you can appreciate the lovely views as you climb gently to the highest part of the walk (a mere 254m!) and the church and cemetery of Cazenac, where there are also some old houses.

*The church is worth a visit if it is open – there are interesting modern stained-glass windows painted by Sylvie Gaudin in 1988, depicting local scenes and the life of the farmers in the region – the faces of the men and women are very realistic.*

**11** Continue down to a stone cross (1hr 50 mins) – **here the yellow signs indicate right, which is a longer way round (not really worth taking as mainly woodland)**. Instead turn left, ignoring a yellow cross, and go down the road into a dip and then up again, past the road to Carvès, off right. The yellow splashes reappear as you go gradually down a narrowing road, passing a vineyard to the right and then entering oak, chestnut and wild laburnum woods where there are huge piles of logs. The track comes out by a dog training field (a large sign saying 'Royal Canin') on the right **(the longer path comes in here from the right just before the field)** (2hrs 5 mins).

**12** Turn left along a track (yellow splashes) just opposite the field and continue down through pleasant woodland, always keeping on the main track, which becomes rocky for a while, to reach a T-junction (2hrs 25 mins).

**13** Turn down right, ignoring the almost immediate track to the left, and continue descending to reach fields and a more substantial jeep track. Bear left on this track, which has extended views over fields – quite a change from the preceding woodland! Shortly after the track becomes tarmac and, as you continue down, there is a lovely view of the bridge across the Dordogne – to the right is the white-coloured Château de Monrecours and ahead (beyond the bridge) the Château des Milandes (see walk no.7). When the road arrives at a corner just before the hamlet of Pech you get a breathtaking view left of Beynac, dominated by the castle, the river and also the châteaux of Fayrac and Marqueyssac on the hills beyond (2hrs 40 mins).

**14** At the corner go left down the hillside on a small path to reach the D703 road, which you should cross immediately to get to the narrow pavement the other side (this is a busy road so be careful). Through the trees you can see the swift currents in the water swirling round the side of an island in the river. You reach a sign saying Beynac and then a large parking area on the right by the side of the river. Turn left and walk up through the village to the Le Crouzet parking (3hrs). Alternatively make your way up through the narrow winding cobbled streets to the entrance to the 13th-century castle (see above for details).

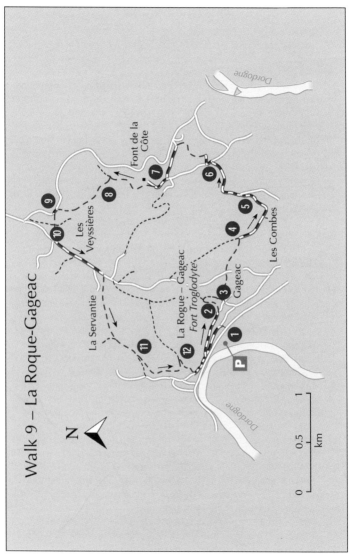

Walk 9 – La Roque-Gageac

# WALK 9
## *Walk around the Village of La Roque-Gageac*

| | |
|---|---|
| **Difficulty:** | Moderate – some upward climbs on easy paths |
| **Time:** | 3hrs 10 mins plus time to visit the village and/or take a boat ride |
| **Length:** | 8.8km |
| **Map:** | Cartes IGN 2036 ET Top 25 Sarlat/Souillac/Vallée de la Dordogne 1:25,000 |
| **Depart from:** | Park near the war memorial opposite a hotel |
| **Signposting:** | Good – yellow splashes |

Squeezed between towering cliffs and the waters of the Dordogne, the medieval village of La Roque-Gageac is one of the most visited villages in France. The walk is best done out of season, although once away from the narrow cobbled streets you will meet hardly anyone. The village houses cling perilously to the rocky cliffs bordering the river, and you wonder how on earth our ancestors managed to build them there in the first place.

The cylindrical tower of the Tarde manor dominates the brown stone roofs huddling under the rock face at the eastern end of the village, and at the western end the Château de Malatrie, perched on a rock, adds to the overall charm of the site. It looks convincingly like the 15th-century original, but was in fact reconstructed in 1926 by the French ambassador to London. Because of its thick ramparts, now destroyed, the village was never taken by the English during the Hundred Years' War and belonged to the Bishop of Sarlat.

To get the best views take a trip along the Dordogne on one of the typical flat-bottomed boats called *gabares,* which were the only means of transport before the railways were built at the beginning of the 19th century. The journey takes an hour and there is an English commentary (albeit not easy to understand). You can see the gash in the cliff face where in 1957 a part of the cliff fell and destroyed all the houses at one end of the village.

### How to get there (from Sarlat)
Take the D57 signposted Bergerac and then at a roundabout bear left on the D46 signposted La Roque-Gageac. Follow this road for 10km and then turn right on

The village of La Roque-Gageac

the D703 for 3km into the village. Park on the left-hand side beside the river where there is a war memorial (cost is 2 euros per day).

## Directions

1   With the river behind you turn right out of the parking, cross the road and go back the way you came into the village, past a tennis court. Cross some waste ground and turn up a short track to reach the road, where you turn left (here you see your first yellow splash). You are now walking through the upper part of the village past a small church, left (dated 1709), and through the *jardin exotique. The vegetation is really tropical down this narrow cobbled street – passion fruit, bananas, numerous species of palms, purple flowering morning glory and even a mandarin tree – a real micro-climate, as the plants are protected by the tall cliffs behind and the houses in front.* At a fork go right upwards towards the Fort Troglodytique ('underground fort'). Just before the porch of the Manoir de Tarde turn up right on a narrow cobbled street following yellow splashes. **Quick detour: go through the porch and you will see the entrance to the Fort Troglodytique on the right and stairs leading up to the caves – look upwards to appreciate the towering cliffs above with their gaping holes, the dwellings of primitive man and afterwards used as a refuge by the villagers in times of war. Visits possible from April to November.** The street is too narrow for cars and is lined with old houses, some of them built right into the cliff face (15 mins).

2   Just before the road starts to descend turn up to the left on a stony track, past the house of Haut La Maison. The path continues fairly flat round the contour of the hill in a U-shape through yew trees and bushes with an old wall on the left covered in ivy. There is a path up to the left, which is a shorter walk round La Roque-Gageac. From here the path goes downwards to meet more houses at a place called Gageac (25 mins).

3   Turn up left by a high wall onto a narrow road (yellow splashes). It goes steeply upwards (ignore road down to the right), turning into a jeep track after the last house and then goes into woodland with crumbling, low ivy-covered walls each side to reach another road. Cross the road and continue upwards on the same type of path bearing to the right round the hillside to meet another road 10 mins later (45 mins).

4   Turn right on this flat, straight, unpaved road bordered by holm oaks, which is the old Roman road from Sarlat to Gourdon – *one can just*

*imagine the Roman soldiers tramping along here in their heavy boots with breastplates clinking!* The road bends gently to the left and there is a beautiful view of the Dordogne valley and surrounding countryside as you continue to an intersection by a large modern house ahead.

5   Turn left towards Les Combes Haut past a *gîte rural* to the right and another big house up left. The road descends into a valley, bending right as it descends and narrows through high banks (ignore road up right). You reach a T-junction at an ugly farm, La Ferme de Labro, where there are huge wire cages full of dried maize to feed the animals and lots of sheds (1hr 10 mins).

6   Turn left and then turn right opposite the farmhouse (*foie gras* for sale). Continue up the road for about 100m and when it curls round right take a path to the left signed Font de la Côte where there are yellow splashes. The raised path goes round the side of a bank and wood, right, and there is a field and later a young walnut orchard to the left. It climbs slightly and then levels out, bearing round to the left to meet a road by a large modern house (1hr 20 mins).

7   Turn down left to reach a T-junction. Turn right on a road going into a narrow combe (small valley), and where it goes up right towards the abandoned farm of Font de La Côte keep up left by a big fir tree on a narrow track bordered by tumbledown walls and woodland with a large field at the bottom of the valley.

8   After the second field by some pines turn up left, signposted Les Veyssières. **Careful – this is not immediately obvious and there are yellow splashes continuing straight**. This is a long, sunken, leafy path where there is lots of ivy, going gently upwards out of the combe through tall chestnut and oak trees to reach a road by a sign 'Prieuré Les Veyssières'.

9   Turn left, and after a few metres turn left again to cross a large field reaching a track (left is marked 'Proprieté Privée', and is another entrance to the Prieuré). Cross the track and follow the pylons across another field to reach the Roman road again (2hrs).

10  Turn left and continue along the straight road, following a sign to Les Bouygues and ignoring a turning right signposted La Roque-Gageac. **Careful** – turn right into chestnut woods just before you see a road coming

in from the left sign-posted Pech Sourbier. The track does a zig-zag and then goes along the side of the hill, where there is a shallow depression down right (Combe de Glary). The track comes to a field, with the farm of La Servantie over on the right, and then starts to descend through tall woodland on a very straight ancient mule path bordered by tumbledown mossy walls. You reach a wider track by a fence and a badly kept vegetable garden. Continue straight till you reach a jeep track by a clearing (2hrs 25 mins).

*Metal knight, part of the ironwork display near La Roque-Gageac*

11  Go up left on a track where it says 'Voie sans issue' (do not go down the jeep track, right) and continue going upwards and round a wide curve where there is a lovely view of the Dordogne river and the château at La Roque-Gageac (*pity about the telephone wires in the way*). The track continues round to pass an amazing display of ironwork in front of a small house in the form of a bird, crab, knight on horseback and other shapes (2hrs 45 mins).

12  A few minutes later go obliquely right to descend through woods on a wide rocky track bordered with ivy-covered walls to reach the road on the edge of the village. Turn left and make your way down into the village and the road along the edge of the river. Turn left and continue along to the car park (3hrs 10 mins).

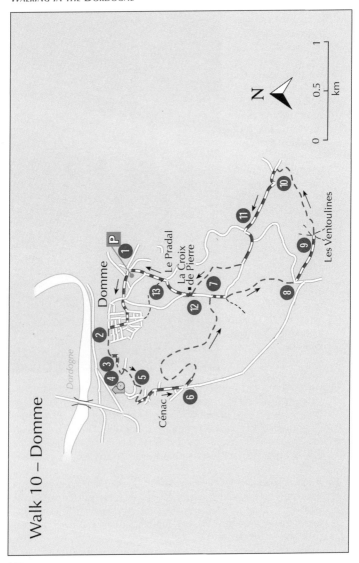

Walk 10 – Domme

# WALK 10
## *La Bastide de Domme*

| | |
|---|---|
| **Difficulty:** | Easy up-and-down walk round a medieval village |
| **Time:** | 2hrs 45 mins/3hrs plus time to look round Domme |
| **Length:** | 8.9km |
| **Map:** | Cartes IGN 2037 Série Bleu Ouest Domme 1:25,000 |
| **Depart from:** | Free car park outside village |
| **Signposting:** | Good – follow yellow splashes, but remember that the variants and shortcuts also have yellow splashes |

This walk starts from another attractive medieval village, which is situated on a bluff with beautiful views of the Dordogne river. Like other villages in the area it is popular with tourists, especially in the high season, which one should try and avoid.

Domme is a *bastide* (fortified village) encircled by ramparts and is entered through an ancient archway, the 13th-century Porte des Tours flanked by guard towers. It was originally built by Philip the Bold in 1281 and, despite its fortifications, was captured many times by the English during the Hundred Years' War. During the Reformation the Huguenots under their leader Geoffroi de Vivans captured it. The soldiers climbed the cliffs and woke up the sleeping inhabitants with a fanfare of drums!

The focal point of the village is the Place de la Halle surrounded by some lovely old buildings. It gives onto the Bélvèdere de la Barre, a walkway with panoramic views of the river below. Once renowned for its surrounding vineyards, the wines being sent as far off as Asia, the vines were destroyed by disease in 1865 and have never been successfully replanted.

### How to get there (from Sarlat)
Take the D57 from Sarlat and then bear left on the D46. At Vitrac turn left over the river on the D46e towards Domme. Before the entrance to the village follow signs left to 'Parking gratuit' (free parking) – 11km from Sarlat.

### Directions

1  Turn left out of the parking the way you came in, where there are yellow

103

*Medieval archway, Domme*

splashes, and walk up the road, following all signs to the centre of the village. Go through the archway Porte des Tours of the old ramparts and bear left following signs to the Tourist Bureau to reach the Grand Rue. Turn up right on a narrow street lined with souvenir shops leading to the large square called Place de la Halle. Go past the Tourist Bureau and church to reach the Bélvèdere de la Barre and Public Gardens. Take time to look around. (This is not, however, included in the timing of the walk. If you make your way directly to the Jardins Publiques and the lovely outlook over the River Dordogne it takes 15 mins.)

2    At the statue of Jacques de Maleville, a local dignitary and holder of the Legion of Honour who was one of the founders of the civil code ('code civile'), turn left and walk down the park enjoying the wonderful views of the Dordogne on the right, with the cliffs towering above the village of La Roque-Gageac on the horizon. Continue down the Promenade de la Barre to reach a small parking and look-out area (esplanade de Jubilé). Go through a small hedge to the lower part of the park, where there is an orientation map next to a tall iron cross (20 mins).

3    With your back to the orientation map walk out of the garden gates and turn down right on the narrow Rue du Vieux Moulin following yellow splashes (ignore a track to the left). A few minutes later you arrive at the restored old mill called Vieux Moulin du Roy and a house called Pugnère, which is situated on the old *citadelle* of Campreal, behind which was the original village of Domme with its château dating from 1438. *The old mill used to be a museum of Périgord Noir but was destroyed during the Second World War – the museum was restored to its original function as a mill in 1950.*

4    Take the narrow lane down left, clearly indicated with yellow splashes. After about 70m turn right down a short, steep grass slope and continue down the narrow path with an ivy-covered wall on the right and a low wall on the left to meet a road. There is a good view of the shallow Cénac valley with houses and an old priory (30 mins).

5    Turn down right for 150m and then left on a corner by a house and a creeper-covered electricity pole. This narrow path winds down the hillside on old terraces and past gardens of houses. There is a good view of the shallow Cénac valley and village with an old priory. You reach a road and houses. Bear left to another road, where you go down left between the village houses of Cénac following yellow splashes to reach a big open

Domme village, with ruins of ramparts in the background

parking area with a large old house, left, which is the school (45 mins). Continue straight through the parking past a *lavoir* (old village washing trough) and follow the straight road indicating Ventoulines. **Do not turn to the left (signposted La Fontaine de Font-Giran) on a narrower road where there are also yellow splashes as this is a variant of the walk**. Walk on till you come to a sign to La Borie opposite a narrow road (45 mins).

6   Turn left where there are some new houses. After the last house the road becomes a track going through fields and woods. Keep straight, ignoring a track down left to a tobacco barn, on a wide track up through beech, chestnut and oak trees. *In early June the author saw a number of orchids, including the delicate yellow butterfly orchid and the rare lizard orchid.* The track does two U-turns, the second round a small valley. Follow yellow splashes, ignoring any tracks going off, to reach another narrow road opposite a football field (1hr 15 mins).

7   Go up the hill right to a second small crossroads (left is signposted Cénac and St Martial Nd). Go straight across and down; the road becomes a jeep track after the last house. Along here there is a sign, right, 'Refuge des Oiseaux' (*never seen that before – I wonder if the birds know it!*). The track undulates through woods and across a shallow valley. Keep to the main path, ignoring any tracks right which are private entrances, to reach a third crossroads at a paved road (1hr 35 mins).

8   Go straight across following the sign to Les Ventoulines and passing new houses. The road goes gently upwards, and from here you have a lovely

view of Domme sitting on its hump above the Yeuses forest one side and rolling countryside on the other. The road goes around a holiday centre with small cabins called Les Ventoulines. Continue on, following yellow splashes and ignoring two tracks coming in from the right (yellow crosses) up a short slope with small chalets on the left.

**9** At the last chalet go straight on a jeep track, still going upwards through chestnut woodland, brambles and juniper bushes. When the trees clear you find you are on a small plateau with eight huge discs over on the right. This is a military zone and there are notices along the side of the path saying it is a private zone and no photographs are allowed. The path reaches a narrow road (2hrs).

**10** Turn down left and continue with occasional houses each side and nice views until you meet a T-junction at the bottom of the slope (2hrs 15 mins).

**11** Turn left and continue down the road for 200m. Go down right, signposted Maisonneuve, Lacombe, Côte de Byne, and right again at a house with a lion on the gate. The route becomes a rough jeep track after the last house and at the bottom of the slope goes into a field. Traverse the field and turn left on a grassy track bordered by a low wall right and brambles to the left (2hrs 25 mins).

**12** At a T-junction turn right to an intersection called La Croix de Pierre (there is a stone cross here – hence the name) (2hrs 35 mins). Go right on the wider road (do not go to La Colombier) following yellow splashes (*this is apparently an old tramway but there is no indication of it*).

**13** Continue up the road for a few minutes and then turn left by a high hedge. **Note:** if you continue on the road (ignoring yellow crosses) this will take you to the parking area outside the village (turn off the road up right where it says 'Centre Village') (2hrs 45 mins).
    **If you wish to end up in the village itself do not continue on the road but turn left again almost immediately onto a wide grassy track following yellow splashes.** Cross a road and follow a sign uphill to the Porte de la Combe (there is a house on the right). At the Porte de la Combe turn left for Porte Dolbos or go straight on for Porte des Tours. At an intersection turn right onto Rue Porte des Tours to return to free car park at the bottom (3hrs).

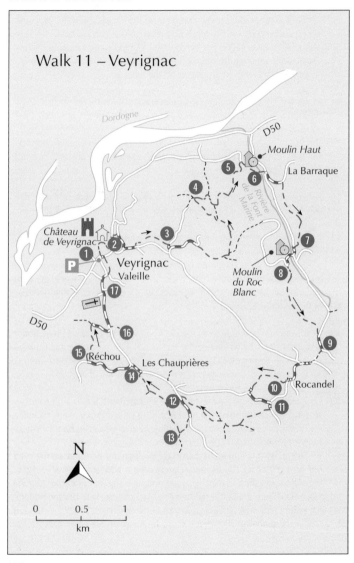

# Walk 11 – Veyrignac

Dordogne

D50

*Moulin Haut*

La Barraque

Rivière de la Font Marine

Château de Veyrignac

Veyrignac
Valeille

*Moulin du Roc Blanc*

D50

Les Chauprières

Réchou

Rocandel

N

0          0.5          1
km

# WALK 11
## *Les Hauts de Veyrignac*

| | |
|---|---|
| **Difficulty:** | Easy up-and-down walk |
| **Time:** | 3hrs 50 mins plus time to visit the Château de Fenelon – 4km from Verignac |
| **Length:** | 12.7km |
| **Map:** | Cartes IGN 2036 ET Top 25 Sarlat/Souillac/Vallée de la Dordogne 1:25,000 |
| **Depart from:** | Parking on the left at the entrance to Veyrignac village |
| **Signposting:** | Good – yellow splashes all the way round but follow them carefully. There are so many turnings onto roads, through woods, etc, that if you miss one you could get lost! |

A pleasant, undulating walk through woods and along the sides of shallow wood-ringed valleys with the occasional hamlet and pretty mill to ring the changes. There is also countless road hopping, which is inevitable in this region. You are very near the Dordogne river, but unfortunately you never see it except when you cross it on the way to Verignac, which is an unassuming small village nestling around a decaying Romanesque church. The château, which overlooks the Dordogne, is in private hands and cannot be visited, although the walk takes you by the gates. Built in the 17th century on the foundations of an earlier building, it was burnt to the ground in 1944. Now fully restored, it has a rather severe aspect with two symetrical towers and a slate roof.

The Château de Fenelon is 4km further on from Veyrignac, near the village of Ste-Mondane. It looks majestic and solid, sitting on a high terrace surrounded by green fields. Started in the 13th century but rebuilt and added to from the 15th to 17th centuries, the château's thick double walls and corner towers are tempered with mullioned windows, tall chimneys, buttresses and carvings, which give it a fairy-tale look. The château was owned originally by one of the oldest and most aristocratic families in the Dordogne region, namely de Salignac de la Mothe-Fénelon. One of them, François, became a well-known writer in the reign of Louis XIV, and the impressive cedar of Lebanon at the entrance gates was planted on his birth in 1651.

The château is open all year round during January–May. October–December

10.00 to 12.00 and 14.00 to 18.00. June–September 9.30 to 19.00.

### How to get there (from Sarlat)

Take the D704, direction Gourdon (south of Sarlat), for 12km. Shortly after crossing the river turn left on the D50 for 2.5km to Verignac. Park on the left at the edge of the village.

*Pigonnier near Veyrignac*

### Directions

1   Turn left out of the parking and left again at a small stone cross. Go down a narrow lane (you will see your first yellow splash here) and along a wall with attractive houses opposite towards the gates of the Château de Veyrignac. From the gates you can see the imposing building (see above for further details). Continue down the lane bearing right to reach the Romanesque church, which looks rather run down and in need of restoration. Following yellow splashes go right round the side of the church passing a wooden edifice used to raise up the oxen in order to shoe them (*travail à bestiaux*). Walk down another narrow walled lane to reach the D50 again by the old forge, where there is a shield carved in the wall showing pliers, a hammer and an anvil (10 mins).

2   Turn left and after 100m turn right down a grassy slope to reach a stone spring at the bottom of the dip. *This looks most strange as it is a large, partially walled enclosure with old stone steps going down each side to a door in a stone arch, from which one presumes the water came.* Following a yellow splash turn right and climb out of the dip to reach a narrow paved road at a T-junction where there is the stone tower of a *pigonnier* (dovecote) in the field in front.

   Turn right and shortly afterwards, at another T-junction, turn left upwards towards the hamlet of Vigier. Just after a small house (larger house up on the right) turn down to the left passing by the garage to descend into a small valley. Cross the field at the bottom of the valley and go up through woodland to reach another road.

3   Turn right for about 100m and then up left again past a house being restored to reach a hairpin bend (30 mins). Leave the road and continue straight on a stony track climbing up gently through woodland. Ignore any tracks coming in from the right (most of them marked with yellow crosses). At a fork go left. The track levels out and continues through stunted green oaks and bushes with good views over to the left. Continue on for about 15mins entering taller woodland.

4   **Careful** – after a gentle bend to the right look carefully for a yellow splash on a tree, left (not obvious), indicating a narrower bushy track going down to the right (50 mins) which descends into chestnut woods to shortly reach a T-junction. Here you go up right and then down to reach a fork, where you go left (no splashes). Shortly after at another T-junction keep left. **Look attentively for the yellow splashes as they are not easy to see.** Continue downwards to go along the side of a shallow valley through taller chestnut trees with fields on the left through the trees. Keep on the main path going down past two fields on the right to come out of the woods where there is a good view. The path bends right and then left through the fields to reach a paved road (1hr 5 mins).

*Château Fenelon*

**5** Turn right and, ignoring another road (to Redon) coming in from the right, descend into La Font Marine valley. You pass a tastefully restored mill called Moulin Haut, with its attractive millpond covered with water lilies on the other side of the road, where you can see the sluice gates. The water goes under the road and continues down the side of the house to eventually join the Dordogne. Just past the mill is a wider road running along the valley.

**6** Cross the road and, following the sign 'Pech d'Estève', go up a steep slope towards La Barraque farm; there is a good view right down to the very wooded and rather gloomy Font Marine valley. **Careful** – just before you get to the farm buildings at the top of the slope, and immediately before a tall conifer on the right (there is also a sign 'Ralentissez enfants'), turn right on a narrow path (not easy to see the yellow splash). There is a dilapidated building behind the tree to the left as you turn. You enter stunted oak forest again as you walk round the flank of the Pech de Courbet (*'pech' is the local word for a low ridge or summit – and they are low in the Dordogne – every wood seems to be a Pech of one sort or another!*). There are good views along here as the bushes become more stunted. The path

*Moulin du Roc Blanc*

bends to the right downwards to fields at the bottom of the valley and a long, barn-like structure. Turn sharply right past a smelly slurry pit through open fields and woodland to reach a road by tall poplars at the bottom of the Font Marine valley once again (1hr 40 mins).

**7** Turn left along the road till you reach the small house of the Moulin du Roc Blanc. Turn right on the narrow road between the mill and the millpond. There are cascades of flowers all around and it is a particularly attractive spot. Continue up the road past another house and pond.

**8** At a hairpin bend (big yellow arrow on a rock) go straight on a jeep track through woodland – there is a small wooden house in the trees, left, and then a newer, bigger one further along. The path continues along the side of the wood and on the left are the fields of the Font Marine valley. It is a pretty path with lots of low, mossy walls and incredible clusters of shiny yellow mushrooms in the autumn. Keep going straight to reach a road at the end of the valley (2hrs).

**9** Turn right for 100m, and just before going round a left-hand corner look for a turning to the right at the end of a field with a yellow splash on a tree further on. **Careful, this is easy to miss.** The sunken path goes up between high rocky walls to another paved road.

   Turn right, passing in front of a house called Le Ponchet to reach a fork. Go up left towards the hamlet of Rocanadel and keep on the road rounding a corner, right, where there are two houses. *There is a 15th-century château here, but apart from a tower sticking out of the trees you cannot see it.*

**10** **Careful** – bear right on a grassy path just after a track coming in from the right and before a yellow cross on a telephone pole (2hrs 10 mins). Continue through a field and vegetable garden to reach woodland followed by tall pines and a small vineyard to the right. Keep straight when a track comes in from the right and continue skirting the wood. The track becomes paved at a very smart private house and continues down, bearing right to a stone cross, where you go left.

**11** Turn right at a subsequent T-junction (ignore the signpost to Rocanadel to the left) and continue for about 50m, turning down right onto a grassy jeep track. There are large open fields here and you are in another shallow valley surrounded by woodland. Keep on the sandy jeep track skirting the fields and ignore any tracks coming in. At a fork go left and enter wood-land to reach a road again (2hrs 45 mins).

12  Go down left for 200m and turn right on a wide jeep track through wood-land; there are lovely fields on the left. **Careful** – as you go round a corner which seems to go into fields, go steeply up to the right over a tree-covered hill. The track is bordered by tumbledown stone walls and there are green fields beyond in the valley. You reach a T-junction (3hrs).

13  Turn right and continue by fields where there is a high bank to the right. A few minutes later go up right on a narrow path (yellow splashes) through oak woods. Shortly afterwards you arrive at a T-junction in front of a wooden tobacco barn at Les Chauprières.

14  Turn left and a few minutes later take another road up left, direction La Barthe (which you never reach), to arrive at a small group of houses called Réchou. Continue through the hamlet on the road, which then winds down through fields and woods.

15  **Careful** – look for a tall poplar tree on the right at the edge of a large field and then a yellow splash on a telephone pole, left, indicating a jeep track off to the right. Go right round the big field and beside woodland to reach a T-junction at Labarthe. Turn right past a new house and walk down, bearing round to the left to reach a wider road (3hrs 35 mins).

16  Go left and continue past a cemetery and new houses. Go straight when a road comes in from the left by a barn with horses to the right to enter the hamlet of Valeille.

17  Bear right after the barn and then almost immediately left behind the houses (yellow splashes). It is a charming hamlet with lots of flowers. Follow the yellow splashes carefully as you turn right between low stone walls and then left round the outside of the houses passing a fig tree to reach the D50 beside the school. Go left and continue (the war memorial is up left) to the car park of Veyrignac on the right (3hrs 50 mins).

# WALK 12
## *Roc de Monges near St-Sozy*

| | |
|---|---|
| **Difficulty:** | Medium but short – there is one steep rocky climb of around 100m. Not to be done in wet conditions. |
| **Time:** | 2hrs 30 mins |
| **Length:** | 7.5km |
| **Map:** | Cartes IGN 2136 ET Top 25 Rocamadour/Padirac/Vallée de la Dordogne 1:25,000 |
| **Depart from:** | Parking area opposite the church at St-Sozy |
| **Signposting:** | Good – follow yellow signposts and splashes |

A really beautiful walk along the Roc de Monges cliffs south of the quaint little village of St-Sozy – the views of the Dordogne and the surrounding countryside are outstanding. There is some scrambling over rocks and a short, stiff climb up to the top, but nothing at all difficult. Even young children could do it, and it is well worth the effort!

### How to get there (from Souillac)
Take the D703, direction motorway, and at a roundabout near a large viaduct go left on the D803, direction Martel. After 5km make a right-hand turn onto the D15, direction Saint Sozy, 5km. In the village, park in the square opposite the church (11km from Souillac).

### Directions

1  With your back to the church, walk by the war memorial and a round stone tower to go straight up a narrow street where there are steps (yellow splashes at the start) and turn left, direction Blanzaguet (straight up is sign-posted 'Pech Grand'). Continue on through some attractive houses to reach the D15 (5 mins).

2  Go straight across (there is a cul de sac sign), ignoring a track left, up through woods on a sunken stony track. Go left where there is a yellow arrow indicating 'Deviation provisoire Blanzaguet' joining a track coming

115

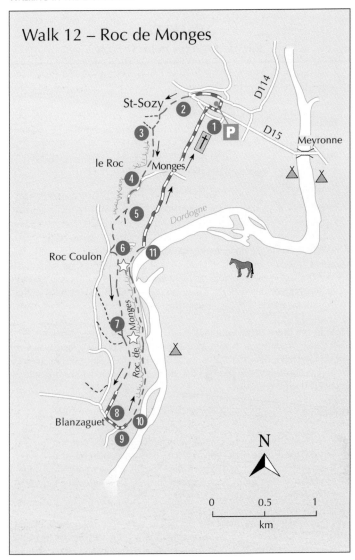

# Walk 12 – Roc de Monges

St-Sozy

le Roc

Monges

Roc Coulon

Roc de Monges

Blanzaguet

Meyronne

Dordogne

D114

D15

N

| 0 | 0.5 | 1 |

km

in from the right and go up a short, very steep, wide track which circles round to the right. Look for a a yellow arrow which takes you off left and left again to reach another U-turn. On this turn look for another arrow indicating left again on a narrow track going over a low wall to reach the original path (20 mins). **Follow the yellow arrows carefully till you get to the proper path again – this strange deviation could be temporary.**

3   Turn left (there is a sign indicating the end of the provisional path). You are walking along the flank of a tree-covered hill and you see your first expansive view of the valley below. Above, through the trees, you can see dramatic rocky cliffs. The track descends through woodland, reaching a narrow road at the attractive hamlet of Monges (30 mins).

4   Turn right and continue, crossing over a narrow stream where there is an ancient wash trough. You are on the floor of the valley with open fields to the left. The paved road becomes a grassy track, but after a couple of minutes, beyond a house on the left, take a narrow path up to the right indicating Roc de Coulon – **careful, this is not easy to see.**

5   This is a narrow stony path going up steeply through tall beech and oak trees and then through higher dense bushes, mainly boxwood. Very little sun reaches this slope, so many of the stunted trees are covered with moss

*View from Roc de Monges, St-Sozy*

and lichen. After about 15mins there is a ledge out to the left where you get your first view of the river (45 mins). *This is an excellent place for a picnic, but be careful as there is an abrupt drop which you cannot see because of the bushes.* Continue on upwards to further views and you can see ponds in the valley below (actually a water purifiying plant). The narrow path emerges abruptly on to a jeep track at the top – further over on the right is a road (55 mins).

6   Turn left towards a radio mast, which is the Roc Coulon – there is an orientation table here and you can admire the fantastic view and put a name to the hills and villages in the valley below (you can see the cliffs of the Mont Mercou, left – see walk no.13). Return to the jeep track behind the radio mast and turn left. The track starts to go down and there are sweeping views in all directions as you go by open pastureland and then stunted woodland and boxwood to reach a junction by a small vineyard (1hr 10 mins).

7   Go straight on down on a wider jeep track (ignoring other tracks coming in) past a vineyard, left, and a walnut orchard to the right as you continue along the side of a shallow wooded valley. There are extensive views of the wooded countryside to the right and the cliffs bordering the meandering Dordogne river. The track becomes paved at the first house on the outskirts of Blanzaguet, and shortly afterwards you come to a T-junction in the village (1hr 25 mins).

8   Go left (there is a stone cross here dated 1838), following a sign 'Saint Sozy par Falaise' (*falaise* means cliffs) and continue through the rather straggly village which has new houses as well as old, passing a *travail à bestiaux* (a wooden apparatus used for raising the bullocks in order to shoe them) to reach a fork.

9   Turn up left following yellow splashes. (**If you want to see the 12th-century chapel go down to the right, but you will be lucky if you find it open. There is the compensation of a lovely view of the Château de Belcastel on a rocky promotory on the other side of the Dordogne.**) The path goes past houses and bears up left by an iron cross (straight on is a house). It continues between two houses, the one on the left being an old barn with a watersource, and narrows into a path by a fir tree, left, and a laurel hedge, right (no immediate yellow splashes) (1hr 30 mins).

*Walking towards St-Sozy*

**10** This narrow bushy path (mind the stinging nettles in summer) goes back along the flank of the hill towards St-Sozy, but lower down. It undulates along with the wooded hillside down on the right and the rocky overhang of the cliffs towering above. Through the bushes you get the occasional glimpse of the Dordogne below. The path continues along underneath the impressive cliffs and grottos finally reaching an *abri historique* (historical site) which is a huge stone archway into a dramatic overhanging grotto, an original dwelling of prehistoric man. Now you are gently descending towards the river.

**Careful** – just before a fence over the path go up to the left over a short slope of scree to scramble over a rock (wonderful view from here) to scramble down steep steps on the other side (this diversion is caused by a small landslide). The path starts to descend and there are some medium-steep steps with a hand rail one side – soon you are level with the river flowing on the right. Continue to reach an open green field with the fenced-in small ponds you saw from above on the outward journey (2hrs).

**11** Continue along the fence left to reach a road. It curves left away from the river through maize fields and walnut orchards. Go straight at a crossroads (Monges to the left) and continue down the delightfully flat road through the scattered houses of La Curade. Ignore a road coming in from the right and continue straight by a tall hedge to reach the St-Sozy road. Turn right to reach the church and village square (2hrs 30 mins).

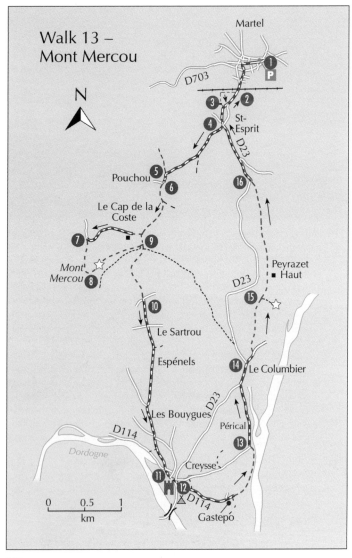

Walk 13 –
Mont Mercou

N

Martel

D703

St-Esprit

Pouchou

Le Cap de la
Coste

Mont
Mercou

Peyrazet
Haut

D23

Le Sartrou

Espénels

Le Columbier

Les Bouygues

D23

Pérical

D114

Dordogne

Creysse

Gastepó

D114

0   0.5   1
km

# WALK 13
## *Circuit round Mont Mercou near Martel*

| | |
|---|---|
| **Difficulty:** | Easy walk with no great height gain |
| **Time:** | 4hrs plus extra time to explore the village |
| **Length:** | 16.3km |
| **Map:** | Cartes IGN 2136 ET Top 25 Rocamadour/Padirac/Vallée de la Dordogne 1:25,000 |
| **Depart from:** | Roundabout at the top of Martel village |
| **Signposting:** | Yellow splashes and GR red/white splashes where applicable. Ignore orange splashes. |

Martel is a very attractive medieval village with an old covered market and seven towers – it is worth taking time to stroll around the narrow cobbled streets with their fascinating old doorways and mullioned windows. One almost expects to see an armoured knight dashing through on a white charger to add to the atmosphere! It is said that the village was founded by a certain Charles Martel ('martel' being another word for 'marteau' – 'hammer' in English), who, after having stopped the Arab invasion at Poitiers in 732, followed them to Aquitaine to defeat them a few years later. To commemorate his victory against the 'infidels' he built a church, from which sprang the village of Martel, whose emblem is three hammers.

Prince Henry, the second son of Eleanor of Aquitaine and Henry II, was suddenly taken ill and died here in 1183, shortly after having plundered the famous shrine of Rocamadour and taken away sackfuls of treasure. Many people thought that his sudden death was heavenly punishment for a sacrilegious crime.

### How to get there (from Souillac)
Follow signs to A20 direction Brive/Martel. At a roundabout by a high viaduct (2.1km from Souillac) turn left on the D703 to Martel. There is plenty of parking (outside the high season) down the main street on the left – 13km from Souillac.

### Directions

1   Make your way to the roundabout at the top of the village and take the D23 road to the left signposted to the motorway and Souillac. Go down

the hill and at a major crossroads at the bottom go straight across. As the road continues out of the village you see your first red/white splash of the GR and a yellow splash. The road goes over a small railway line (fenced off to the left but beyond is a small station). *It is possible to take an hour and a half train ride on the small steam train called 'Truffadou'. For further information tel. 05.65.37.35.81.*

2   Shortly afterwards take a turning to the right where there is a sign saying 'Chemin Pédestre – Départ du Tour du Martel' (10 mins) on a jeep track (the GR goes straight up the road but you join it later). The track passes the old village *lavoir* (washing trough) on the left, then allotments, and becomes grassier as it bends to the left and starts to go upwards between hedges to reach a T-junction. Go right past a field of *puits* (wells) to a narrow paved road (15 mins).

3   Go right and continue upwards to reach another road a few minutes later, where you turn left and almost immediately come to an intersection called St-Esprit on the map.

4   Turn right, direction Sargunat and Pouchou – there is a lovely view of Martel behind you. Keep to the narrow paved road through open fields and vines and ignore a jeep track off left as you turn a corner. The road

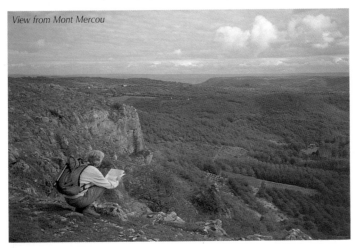

*View from Mont Mercou*

goes up and then down through stunted oak wood, with houses up on the hill ahead, to arrive at a T-junction.

5     Turn left following the sign 'Pouchou' and yellow splashes (30 mins).

6     A few minutes later turn left again (the road goes on to Pouchou) on a *castiné* (in the local dialect this means an unpaved road). There is a sign here indicating Mont Mercou. Keep going on the main track. **Careful** – do not take the track ahead (there is a post box here) where the main track is bearing up to the right. Ignore any subsequent tracks coming in. You are walking through stunted oak trees, bushes and small grassy clearings – there are isolated houses partially hidden in the woods. The track goes down a small incline and then goes up to the right (ignore another track left here). When you reach a farm on the left called Le Cap de la Coste the track becomes paved again. Keep going on the road passing a large house on the left (Jaqueblanc) and continue winding upwards till you see a house on the right (no name on the map) (55 mins).

7     With the house opposite go up to the left on a wide track to reach a large sign in a clearing. Keep going up left to reach the Mont Mercou (alt. 318m), which is a wide escarpment. From here there is a wonderful view of the Dordogne countryside, woodlands and fields dotted with houses and farms. You can see the cliffs bordering the Dordogne, though you cannot see the river itself. This is the ideal place to stop and have a picnic (1hr 5 mins).

8     Turn left on a narrow stony path (there is a yellow splash on a rock), which goes along the edge of the slope with beautiful views to the right. The path traverses the hill quite steeply in places (be careful in wet weather as the stones can be slippery here), and passes through stunted woodland and glades to reach a T-junction at the end of the slope (1hr 20 mins).

9     Turn left following yellow splashes on a tree and almost immediately you reach a jeep track at another T-junction, where you turn down right. **Careful** – shortly after there is a path down to the right on a corner (yellow splashes and an orange cross) (1hr 25 mins). **Note: If you go straight down the jeep track, bearing off left on the GR46, this is a shorter route back – not done by author.** Go down this steep narrow path through stunted woodland passing a disused quarry to arrive at the bottom of the valley, where there is an orchard of walnut trees and cultivated fields (a huge asparagus field to the left) at a paved crossroads (1hr 35 mins).

**10** Go straight across to another crossroads where you go straight again, direction Creysse (to the left is Le Got and to the right is Boutière). Keep going along this narrow paved road for about half an hour, through the scattered houses of Le Sartrou and Espénels, and avoid any roads coming in. It is delightfully rural countryside with open cultivated fields, walnut trees and woodland always on the horizon – occasionally you catch a glimpse of the cliffs towering above the Dordogne. The road loses height very gradually.

**11** At a fork, where the main road bears off to the left, take the right branch where there is a 'No entry' sign (yellow splashes). Continue till you are walking by a high wall to the right, which is the outskirts of Creysse on the D23. *This is a village which seems to have escaped the 'tarting up' of so many places in the Dordogne valley region – many of the houses are shuttered, but there are still a number of dwellings that have fallen into disrepair and have not yet been snapped up!*

Walk through this delightful little village with the ruins of a 15th-century châteaux and its Romanesque church. Traverse the miniscule main square, past the renovated covered *halles*, where a market takes place once a week in the high season. Bear down to the left and over a small stream by a bridge (Rau de Cacrey) and past a *buvette* (café) to arrive at a road, where there is a peaceful looking Logis de France hotel to the left (Auberge de L'Ile). Go right to an intersection (2hrs 15 mins).

**12** Take the road indicating Gastepo (D114), which passes a camping area and continues through pastureland on the right (a flood plain), where there are tall trees. Keep going on the main track, which goes from paved to jeep track and passes the little hamlet of Gastepo on the left (2hrs 25 mins). You are walking towards Dordogne on a raised track bending to the left with high ivy-covered rocks on one side. Soon you are right by the water, bordered by tall trees, you can appreciate the beauty and tranquillity of this delightfully wide river as it flows past. The wide track stops at a turning point for cars and narrows into a path, this climbs up for a short while through brambles to arrive at two houses. Continue around the side of the first house to meet a narrow road (2hrs 35 mins).

**13** Turn right (over on the left you can see the buildings of an *elevage* and a Nut Research station) and walk past some rather untidy agricultural buildings towards the hamlet of Périca. The river has split, and the narrower tributary is over on the right but not visible through the trees. The road continues flat through cultivated fields of maize and walnut orchards. The

D23 comes in again from the left as you walk along.

**14** At an intersection called Le Columbier, go right on the D43 signposted Gluges (the D23 goes off left) past a house and then look for a well-marked path up left signposted Martel 4.3km, where there are also GR46 red/white splashes (2hrs 55 mins). The wide track is going up and over what is known locally as a *causse*, a flat, open limestone area. This one is covered in bushes and stunted oak trees interspersed with grassland. There are low crumbling stone walls on either side, and it must have been a major highway before the present road was built. Continue upwards for around 15 mins, when the track levels out. Ignore a sign to the right saying 'Fontaine' but continue till you see another sign saying 'Gluges' (3hrs 10 mins).

## Diversion (10mins)

**15** Take this narrow path right and after a few minutes you have a wonderful vista of the Dordogne below with the cliffs bordering the water beyond. *When the author did this walk she had the added bonus of seeing an enormous maze cut into a field of maize below – seen from above it looked a real work of art.* Retrace your steps to the main path.

*View of Dordogne and maze, Martel*

*Housing corn*

16  The track reaches a lovely house (Peyrazet Haut) on the right, which looks deceptively isolated, as the D23 is just over on the left – there is a primitive map of the area here. Keep on the main track (avoid track going down left), which is now quite flat and there are views of surrounding tree-covered hills. Soon there are houses and almost immediately the track joins the D23 (3hrs 30 mins).

17  Turn right and continue along the road passing some nice houses to reach the St-Esprit crossroads passed on the outward journey (see point 3, above). Stick to the road going downwards, crossing the railway tracks to reach Martel village. Retrace your steps to the parking (4hrs).

# WALK 14
## *Walk around the Gouffre de Padirac*

| | |
|---|---|
| **Difficulty:** | Medium – mostly on the flat, but the walk along the ridge has spectacular views |
| **Time:** | 4hrs (from the start of the GR) plus extra time to explore the village of Loubressac and visit the Gouffre de Padirac if open |
| **Length:** | 13.8km |
| **Map:** | Cartes IGN 2136 ET Top 25 Rocamadour/Padirac/Vallée de la Dordogne 1:25,000. A small part of this walk is off the map. |
| **Depart from:** | Parking at the Gouffre de Padirac |
| **Signposting:** | Good in parts – small yellow signs in places. Follow red/white GR splashes and blue/yellow splashes. |

A walk along a flat *causse* (limestone plateau) to reach a charming medieval village. The path along the ridge to Siran is dramatic with beautiful views, so it is worth the effort!

### Gouffre de Padirac

It is worth visiting the Gouffre de Padirac as it is one of the largest *gouffres* (chasms) in France (22km). The tour entails descending by lift into the bowels of the earth and taking a boat along an underground river to see the magnificently illuminated stalactites and stalagmites; all rather exciting! The visit takes about an hour (longer in the high season if you can brave the queues). It is open at the following times:

| | |
|---|---|
| 1st April – 6th July | 9.00–12.00 and 14.00–18.00 |
| 7th – 31st July | 9.00–18.30 |
| 1st – 31st August | 8.30–18.30 |
| | SHUT 2nd November – 1st April. |

Cost 8 euros (adults), 6 euros (children). Remember to take an anorak as it is cold down there! Website: www.gouffre-de-padirac.com; E-mail: info@gouffre-de-padirac.com

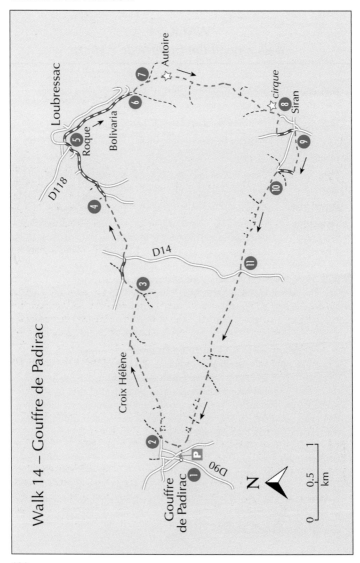

Walk 14 – Gouffre de Padirac

The fortified 15th-century village of Loubressac is dramatically situated on a rocky outcrop overlooking the Bave valley (part of the larger Dordogne valley). From the fortifications you can also see the village of St-Céré, distinguished by its towers, as well as the châteaux of Castelnau and Montal.

Although probably used by locals as a hideaway during the Hundred Years' War, the *gouffre* was explored for the first time in 1889 by Edouard Martel, the famous pot-holer, who lead a further nine expeditions to explore this enormous hole which was opened to the public for the first time in 1899.

The legend of the Gouffre de Padirac is interesting – St Martin was walking in the area looking for souls to convert when he met the devil. They had a conversation and the devil mocked St Martin and challenged him to a contest. The devil hit the ground with his heel and opened up a huge hole (the *gouffre*), challenging the saint to leap across. Without hesitation St Martin made the sign of the cross and kicked his donkey who made a tremendous leap across (the imprint of his hoof can still be seen on the edge of the *gouffre*). The devil was furious that he had lost the contest and flung himself into the hole, and that is why the Gouffre de Padirac is called the entrance to hell!

This walk is best done out of the high season or when the *gouffre* is shut.

## How to get there (from Souillac 35km)

Take the D703 from Souillac to Le-Pigeon. Then turn off right on the D15 crossing the Dordogne river at St-Sozy and continuing till you reach the D673 at Reveillon. Turn left through Alvignac to Padirac, where you turn on the D90 to the Gouffre.

From Souillac there are frequent signs indicating Gouffre de Padirac, so you can't go wrong. The area around the *gouffre* itself has lots of parking, so park as near to the roundabout as possible – there are crowds of people in the high season.

## Directions

1   From the roundabout in the middle of a conglomeration of restaurants, souvenir shops, picnic and parking areas (the *gouffre* itself is to the left), go through the central tarmac parking area to the right of the D90. Look for a GR652 marking on a telephone pole hidden by a 'P' sign on the right of the car park. Turn right on the road and go up a wide gravel track for a few metres following a line of trees and a wall round to the top, where there is a small yellow sign (hard to see) on a tree and more red/white GR splashes. Go left following the GR sign 'Circuit des Merveilles Taillefer' and continue up the track for a few minutes to a junction where the GR652 divides.

Medieval village of Loubressac

2   Turn to the right by a large cultivated field following the sign 'Loubressac 5.2km' on a flat, wide jeep track through open country consisting of small fields of coarse grass dotted with bushes and trees. You are walking on what is known locally as a *causse* (limestone plateau), where the land is used for mainly for sheep rearing, although there are some ploughed fields. Keep to the main track bordered by tumbledown walls, bushes and brambles following the GR splashes. You pass a stone cross on the left (Croix Hélène) in memory of Hélène who was killed here in 1844. *It is a mystery to me why and how a person was killed in such a remote spot.* The track continues down to the right of a shallow tree-covered valley (Pech Sahuc) and then later by an enclosure before meeting a T-junction (35 mins).

3   Turn left till you join a jeep track coming in from the left. Continue on the GR to the right on the now paved road, crossing the D14 a few minutes later onto another track. After climbing gently the mule track undulates along, bordered by crumbling walls, through scattered low woodland to reach another road coming in from the right (1hr).

4   Turn left and then a few minutes later left on a wider road passing the sign saying Loubressac. Continue through scattered private houses (some very

smart), past a stone cross, a caravan park and an old wooden edifice for shoeing oxen (*travail à bestiaux*). At an intersection carry on straight passing the Tourist Bureau on the right to arrive at the main square of Loubressac by a war memorial (1hr 25 mins).

*Take time to stroll round the village with its cobbled streets, lovely old tiled houses and church with wide cupolas. The privately owned 15th-*

*Statue over entrance to church, Eglise St Jean-Baptiste in Loubressac*

century château is perched on the end of the jutting ridge, so has the best views to the west of the Château de Montal, the village of St-Cére, the towers of St-Laurent and the Bave valley.

5   From the square follow round to the right where you get your first panoramic view to the east over the Cère and Dordogne valleys, with the low, tree-covered hills beyond. There is a good view of the Castelnau and Turenne châteaux from here. **Careful** – do not bear down left here on a grassy track with GR splashes which is a variant of the GR652, but go by a crucifix and a sign marked 'sauf riverains' on a narrow road out of the village past the houses of Roque, where there are continuing views. The road continues down past a delightful park of oak trees by a large private house. Further on you pass a large farm on the left called Bolivaria to arrive at a crossroads (1hr 45 mins). **If you do not wish to go across the ridge with its dramatic views turn right here, continuing on the GR, and walk along a jeep track to arrive at the hamlet of Siran (not done by author).**

6   At the crossroads you leave the GR652. Go straight on slightly upwards on a wide gravely track through woods and fields ignoring other tracks coming in. At a corner do not continue round left ('Propriété privée/défense d'entrer') but go straight on a narrow path. There is a notice here warning people that they go on this path at their own risk. **It would appear from the notice that this is a dangerous path, but there should be no problem if you keep to the track on the top of the ridge.** Go through a short stretch of woodland to arrive at the edge of the ridge and an intersection (2hrs).

7   Take the high track up to the right (blue/yellow splashes as you go up this path). **Careful** – do not take the lower one to the right or the one going down left, which goes to the village of Autoire in the valley. **(There is a circuit that goes down to Autoire, to the waterfall and then back up the ridge to Siran but it is somewhat longer.)** The track goes all the way along the rocky, bushy escarpment, sometimes near to the edge and sometimes further away. The view into the valley is spectacular, as you look right down onto the medieval village of Autoire. Where there is a choice of paths, one nearer the edge than the other, keep to the higher path with the yellow and blue splashes which keeps to the top of the ridge. **Always keep to the more defined path along the ridge.** The valley on the left is now deepening into a gorge and there is a road going along the other side. Soon you can see an impressive waterfall falling over the other side of the gorge, La Cascade d'Autoire (2hrs 30 mins).

Further on there is a path going down the ridge in a series of wooden steps signposted Château des Anglais. This is the variant of the GR652 coming up from the village of Autoire. If you want to see the ruins of the château they are about 20 mins down the steep slope, but not really worth the detour.

Continue straight following GR splashes. From here the track becomes wider, going through higher woodland to reach the few scattered houses

*Eastern doorway into the medieval village of Loubressac*

of Siran, beautifully positioned on the side of the ridge. There is a special lookout spot here for people to admire the impressive waterfall on the other side of the valley. Look down and you will see that you are standing above a circle of sheer rock face, called a 'cirque' on the map. The track becomes paved as you enter the few houses of Siran (2hrs 45 mins).

**8**   Turn right following yellow sign Circuit des Merveilles and GR splashes. The road turns into a jeep track to reach a grassy T-junction. Go left ignoring GR cross (you are now off the GR). The path becomes paved at a farm and continues to reach an iron cross at an intersection.

**9**   **Careful** – walk round the cross to the right (wall over on the left) and you will see a yellow wooden man on an oak tree indicating straight down a grassy track. The track reaches another road where you turn right and continue till you see a road coming in from the right (3hrs 5 mins).

**10**  Go up left by a sign saying Loubressac Camping along a narrow track. **Careful** – as there is no proper sign here, though later there are intermittent blue/yellow splashes. This is a long, straight track going up again very gently across the *causse*. There are crumbling stony walls from time to time and pleasant extended views over the uncultivated pastureland dotted with stunted bushes. The path widens to a jeep track when a grassy, undefined track comes in from a field with a ruin on the right (blue/yellow splash here). Go through a wire fence.

**11**  The track crosses the D14, where there is a memorial stone commemorating the parachute descent of 1000 American soldiers to bring supplies and ammunition to the French Resistance on the 14th July 1944 (3hrs 40 mins).

Continue straight, ignoring a track off to the right 5 mins later and subsequent other tracks. After reaching a grassy open area where the views are extended, the track starts to go gently downwards to arrive at the parking area (4hrs).

# WALK 15
## *Walk around the Mills of the Alzou Gorge: Rocamadour*

| | |
|---|---|
| **Difficulty:** | Medium – parts of this walk are steep and there is some scrambling around rocks, which is tricky if the stones are wet. |
| **Time:** | 3hrs 45 mins to the entrance of Rocamadour, plus at least 1hr for looking around the village, climbing the steps to the basilica and walking back to the car |
| **Length:** | 13.6km |
| **Map:** | Cartes IGN 2136 ET Top 25 Rocamadour/Padirac/Vallée de la Dordogne 1:25,000 |
| **Depart from:** | Opposite the Tourist Bureau in L'Hospitalet |
| **Signposting:** | Yellow splashes until you meet the red/white splashes of the GR6. |

A satisfying walk along the rocky Alzou gorge with its many ruined mills in attractive settings at the edge of the water. **Warning:** do not do this walk if there has been lots of rain as the river gets easily flooded and you cannot cross it. It is best done in summer time when the river is dry.

Rocamadour is one of the most visited sites in the whole of France, and has been visited by pilgrims since the 11th century. Somehow it doesn't matter that it is crowded nearly every day of the year, as this holy shrine, despite the abundance of souvenir shops, cafés and hotels, has an air of magic about it. The sudden view of the sinuous line of houses, clinging to the edge of a huge cliff made by the River Alzou, is breathtaking. The buildings are dominated by the huge St-Sauveur Basilica with its many chapels, separated from the village itself by an impressive stone stairway, and on the crest itself is the imposing château. How and why such a place was constructed in such difficult terrain before modern building methods is a mystery and a miracle!

The reason for the religious popularity of Rocamadour is the miraculous statue of the Black Madonna which over the centuries has performed many miracles. In earlier times pilgrims used to climb the long stone staircase on their knees to beg for favours at her shrine in the Notre Dame chapel.

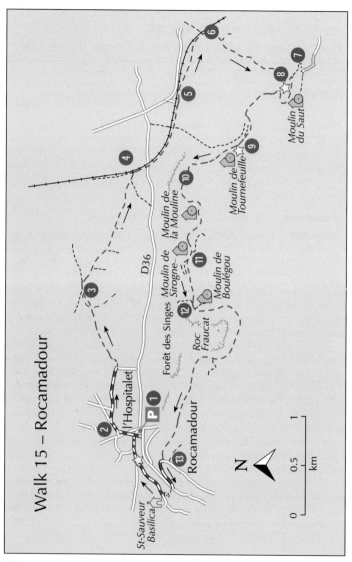

Walk 15 – Rocamadour

## How to get there (from Souillac 26km)

Take the D703, direction motorway Brive/Martel. **Note:** When the new motorway going south opens, it will be easier to take the motorway – Rocamadour is sure to be signposted. At a huge viaduct go left on the D703, direction Martel. Then at Pigeon turn right on the D15 through St-Sozy and over the Dordogne river. Turn right on the D673, direction Rocamadour 5km. The road reaches l'Hospitalet, where you turn up to the right and park opposite the Tourist Bureau. It is a good idea to visit the Tourist Bureau and pick up all the information about Rocamadour.

## Alternative way from Sarlat (58km but quicker)

Take the D704 to Gourdon, and the D801 to Le Vigan. Then take the D673 and N20 to Payrac, and turn right on the D673 to Rocamadour. Continue to L'Hospitalet and its parking.

## Directions

1  Facing the Tourist Bureau go right on the D673 towards a T-junction (right is the D32, direction Toulouse/Gramat/Figeac, and left is the D673A20 to Paris/Brive/Martel/St Céré). Go left and walk past the sign indicating the end of L'Hospitalet.

2  Take the first narrow road to the right by two white/red bollards but no splashes (5 mins). You are on a *causse*, which is a high limestone plateau with fields and pastureland bordered by stone walls or hedges and scattered woodland, mostly oak trees. It is mainly sheep-grazing country but a few crops are grown. Ignore a track coming in from the left and another on the right as you keep to the narrow tarmac road passing a small oak plantation (planted so that when the trees mature they will encourage truffles to grow near the roots) and later a campsite. After a house the road becomes a jeep track and continues between intermittent stone walls, brambles and bushes. Go straight at a small crossroads and continue straight when a track comes in from the left.

3  **Careful** – a few minutes later take the first turning right where you see a yellow splash on a stone 30m up the path (25 mins). Keep going on the main track following yellow arrows on the ground through pastureland and trees, ignoring any joining tracks. The path goes between mossy walls and in and out of woodland to reach a T-junction with the railway lines beyond (45 mins).

*Ruins of the Moulin de Tournefeuille in the Alzou gorge, near Rocamadour*

4   Turn right towards a crossing-keeper's house with the railway line on the left to reach a narrow road (left is a small level crossing and a house). Cross the road onto a wide track following yellow and white arrows, past a big barn, right. Continue with the railway line up on the left to a GR6B signpost indicating straight 'Moulin du Saut 2km and Gramat 7km' (1hr).

5   Do not go left on the jeep track and under the railway bridge but follow the GR splashes straight along a wide jeep track (you can hear the cars on the road over on the left) through fields sown with crops, passing a 'Signal automatique' sign to reach another T-junction with another level crossing to the left (1hr 10 mins).

6   Go right down a stonier shady track descending gently to the start of the Gorges d'Alzou. Following the red/white GR markings (ignore the orange) the path goes along the side of the gorge to reach a dramatic viewpoint. You can see down into the tree-covered gorge below and the dramatic rocky cliffs on the other side. Continue down left on a wide rocky path, which takes you towards the bottom of the gorge (1hr 30 mins).

7   At a GR6 signpost go right towards the Moulin du Saut/Rocamadour. (The sign left indicates Lauzou/Gramat.) You are now on a balcony path above the river which you can see down below on the left for the first time – it goes under rocky cliffs to arrive at the weir of the Moulin de Saut, which was once a mill of some standing. As you walk through the ruins, you can see the old bread oven and the enormous stone mill wheels. There are stone steps going round the different areas, through an ancient archway, and past sinister, dark, dank caverns, which are scary to investigate. In many places the old wooden beams are still standing – it resembles a castle rather than a mere mill. At one place you can see where the river flowed over and down into the mill wheels – there is little water now, and one wonders why the river dried up and whether the lack of water caused the demise of the mills.

8   Shortly after, where the path divides, keep up right away from the river to a lovely viewpoint of the high cliffs on the other side of the gorge. **Caution here,** as the path is high above the gorge and narrow going under rocks. There is a fence to stop people slipping over, though there are plenty of trees! The path starts to wind down through the beech woods and over man-made wooden steps. You reach the bottom of the gorge again and the river, which is dry in places but runs gently in others, creating small pools.

It is a well-trodden path going through delightfully spaced out deciduous woods. The stream goes round a huge rock and the path goes up to the right and round it. **Careful** – the rocks are slippery and you have to pick your way up and down; it is helpful to have long legs here (1hr 55 mins). Continue along with the water on the left as you go deeper into the gorge over tree roots through beech forest.

**9** The track goes up to reach a bridle path coming in from the right. Go left, signposted GR6 Rocamadour 4.5km, to reach the ruins of the Moulin de Tournefeuille where the gorge is wider and there are high cliffs on the other side – a good place for a picnic (2hrs 5 mins).

Continue till the river is in front of you and then cross the river following the GR signs. **Follow all the red/white GR signs along the river indicating when to cross.** You will pass some big, rusty old cauldrons which were formerly used for charcoal gathering.

**10** You reach a wider track bending to the right where there is a GR splash and you go up again on a rather slippery slope to descend to the third mill, called Moulin de la Mouline (2hrs 35 mins). This is a heavily ivy-covered ruin, but you can see some old mill wheels and where the water was diverted into the mill.

**11** Shortly afterwards the path reaches the fourth mill, called the Moulin de Sirogne, and you can see where the river was dammed to divert the water to the mill wheels and the chimney of the ancient bread oven (2hrs 45 mins). You cross an old paved bridge to continue on the other side of the water. The gorge starts to open out now and meets a jeep track coming in from the right. Here there is a notice saying that the path taken was a 'Propriété privée' (private path) and that the owners take no responsibility for any accidents!

**12** Go left on the wide jeep track. **Short detour**: shortly afterwards take a wide, grassy track to the left (no sign) and over a wooden bridge, where you can barely see the ivy-covered ruins of the fifth mill hidden in vegetation, the Moulin de Boulégou. Retrace your steps to the jeep track and continue on. As you turn a corner there is a lovely silhouette of rocky cliffs ahead. The river here becomes more elusive, sometimes hidden in trees, but it continues all the way to Rocamadour. Continuing along the valley bottom the track does a wide circle around the impressive Roc Fraucat – there is another wooden bridge left to a pretty old barn in a field. If you look up ahead you can see a long fence along the bottom of the cliffs, which encloses a Forêt des Singes (monkey park). There are now scree-covered slopes dotted with bushes to the right as you walk along here. You know you are reaching civilisation again as you can see cars going along the road high on the right. Go through a barrier across the jeep track (presumably to stop cars entering).

A park appears on the left with planted trees, and up on the crest of the hill are the first houses of Rocamadour. The jeep track turns into a narrow road, which you go off left on a *passage pietons* (footpath) through the park. You reach an intersection – to the left is signposted Cahors/Couzout, and straight indicates the town (3hrs 30 mins).

**13** Go up right where there is a 'No entry' sign, signposted 'cité/Sanctuaire/Château', and then up right again where there are some steps to reach the 13th-century archway (Porte de Figuier) which is the entrance to the medieval village of Rocamadour (3hrs 45 mins).

**From here you have a choice:** to see the historical Basilica of St-Sauveur and the chapel of Notre Dame, with its famous statue of the Black Virgin (*don't be disappointed – it is very small*), turn left and go through the Porte de Figuier and down the main street which is lined with lovely old houses, cafés and souvenir shops (many of them selling the renowned Périgord *foie gras*). Continue through the second 13th-century archway (Porte Salmon) till you reach the start of the famous holy steps (up right) which in the old days the pilgrims crawled up on their knees saying a prayer at each step. If you do not want to walk up there is a lift. At the end of your visit you will be at the top of the village. To get to L'Hopitalet turn right and walk along the road for about 15 mins.

**If you have already seen the town** turn right on the road instead of going through the archway and walk up the hill, direction L'Hopitalet. Careful where there is a fork – take the narrower road, left, which has a 'No entrance' sign and a white stone cross. You will reach another archway and the old church of L'Hospitalet. Bear left, which takes you through a little park to the parking in front of the Tourist Bureau (15 mins) (not included in the overall timing of the walk).

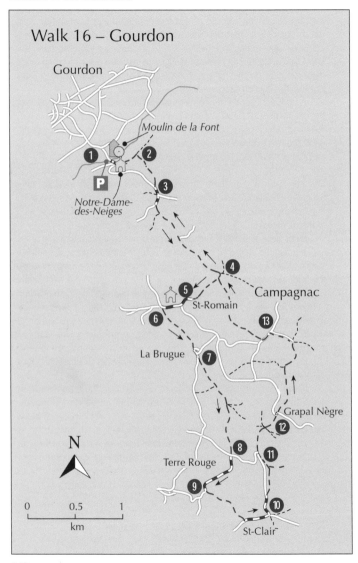

# Walk 16 – Gourdon

Gourdon

*Moulin de la Font*

1

2

P

*Notre-Dame-des-Neiges*

3

4

5

St-Romain

Campagnac

6

13

La Brugue

7

Grapal Nègre

12

N

8

Terre Rouge

11

9

10

St-Clair

0    0.5    1
km

# WALK 16
## *Circuit de Notre-Dame-des-Neiges*

| | |
|---|---|
| **Difficulty:** | Easy walk with no great ups and downs |
| **Time:** | 3hrs 15 mins |
| **Length:** | 11.2km |
| **Map:** | Cartes IGN Série Bleue 2037E Gourdon 1:25,000 |
| | **Note**: the paths are difficult to see on the Série Bleue maps |
| **Depart from:** | Notre-Dame-des-Neiges church near Gourdon |
| **Signposting:** | Start GR64 – then green and orange splashes – not always very consistent or visible |

An easy, undulating walk in the picturesque Bleou valley region, starting from the ancient chapel of Notre-Dame-des-Neiges near Gourdon and continuing through the two attractive small hamlets of St-Clair and St-Romain.

Gourdon, capital of the Bouriane region, is a medieval town perched on a small hill, on the summit of which are the ruins of the former castle. It was destroyed in 1621 when the then Lord of Gourdon got on the wrong side of a dispute between Marie de Medici and her son Louis XIII. The walls were taken down to make a circular road round the town, and Gourdon is now a vibrant centre of the surrounding district, with a music festival in July and August attracting numbers of tourists.

### How to get there (from Sarlat)
Take the D704 from Sarlat signposted Cahors/Gourdon for 25km. When you arrive at Gourdon there is a junction. Take the right-hand fork, signposted Brive/Souillac (left goes to the centre of town). Drive down (one-way system) past the Casino Supermarket on the right. Take the next road left, which is the Rue Jean Moulin, and continue till you come to a T-junction. Turn left (railway bridge on the right) to reach a hamlet, crossing over a small river to the lovely chapel of Notre-Dame-des-Neiges facing an old mill, le Moulin de la Font (1.4km from Gourdon).

There is a notice here saying you are at the chapel in the Vallon de Bleou. If the doors are open it is worth going inside – only the apse remains from the original Romanesque church and there is an altar by Tournier.

*Typical pigonnier in the Dordogne*

**Directions**

1. As you face the chapel go up the narrow road to the left and take the first turning left on a wide track (you are on the GR64 for a short while), where there is a large field left and a pleasant view of the shallow Bleou valley.

2. After a few minutes turn right at a wooden sign indicating St Clair 5km and green and orange markings (the GR64 continues straight). Go up this sunken lane bordered with ivy, through woodland and fields higher up, to meet a narrow road. Turn left to reach scattered houses and an intersection (15 mins).

**3**   Go straight following the sign St-Romain. At a second intersection by a house, left, and a little one on the right continue straight down. The initial jeep track becomes the driveway to a house on the left, but continue straight on a grassy path past a water pump and a telegraph pole with an orange arrow (ignore the green splashes indicating right and left as it is a red herring) and later pass a beautiful renovated barn and house to the right. Cross a narrow road, which is the entrance to the house, and go straight down an attractive lane with a bank one side and woods the other, where there is a lovely view into a shallow valley. The lane undulates along through woods and fields to arrive at a crossroads (35 mins).

**4**   Turn right on a jeep track following green splashes. As the jeep track descends you can see the hamlet of St-Romain ahead in the valley. The track goes by a huge newly built house on the left (not shown on the map) and past a wrought iron cross on a stone pillar before meeting an unpaved road. Turn right (left is the private road to the house, also not on the map) and continue over a bridge and the stream which has been flowing on the left to reach the rather dilapidated church and buildings of St-Romain by a war memorial and junction (45 mins).

**5**   At the junction go right (the green splashes go straight on and it is possible to reach La Bruge by going up this road), and continue till you see an iron cross on the left just before another intersection.

**6**   Turn up left just after the cross (**careful, easy to miss and there are no splashes**) on a narrow path fairly steeply through woods, levelling off as it comes to open pastureland, to reach the tarmac road at La Bruge, which consists of one charming isolated house with barns. You are quite high here and there is a lovely view down the shallow valley behind with the large house passed on the way down to St-Romain (1hr).

**7**   Continue straight on the tarmac road (do not go down left) and shortly after, just as the road bends to the right by a house, go straight on a wide, grassy track (green splashes). You walk through stunted woodland with frequent open glades and shortly after, at the top of a slight rise when the main path curls slightly left, bear off to the right (green splash further up the path on a tree) by an area of chopped down trees – **this is not easy to see**. The track goes slightly downward and curls around the hillside on a low ridge through an old chestnut forest to reach a crossroads (1hr 20 mins).

**8** Cross the road past an old orchard and vineyards to reach another attractive house and the hamlet of Terre Rouge, which consists of a few buildings, a swimming pool and a big ugly barn! As you continue through scattered woodland you get extended views in all directions.

**9** When the road bends to the left at a ruin, right, 10 mins later, take a turning down left on a wide grassy track descending through tall woodland and open areas to the village. There are more views as you get lower and you can see a large house standing alone in the forest on the horizon. Keep on the main path to reach the remote but attractive hamlet of St-Clair at an ugly car dump (1hr 40 mins).

**10** The road passes the renovated market place (*halles*) and leads to the war memorial in front of the old church on the D17. Turn left and walk out of the village. Just after another iron cross and by a house, take the first narrower road up left following orange/green splashes and a sign to Terre Rouge. **Careful here** – shortly after, just before the road starts to go up, bear up right on an overgrown jeep track through woods parallel to the road (1hr 45 mins). **If you miss the jeep track continue on the road till the hairpin bend**.

**11** A few minutes later when the track starts to go round right, bear left on a narrower track – there are splashes on a tree and a large cross on the track ahead. The track goes up through wood by a small tree-covered gully to the right. It comes out near the road at a hairpin bend, but goes back into the woods and up the side of the gully to reach a small grassy plateau with walnut trees. Bear slightly left (do not take the immediate path left) and a few minutes later you reach a T-junction at an unpaved road (2hrs 10 mins).

**12** Turn right and go downwards to meet another road where you turn up right towards the buildings of Grapal Nègre farm. Where the road bends to the right and just before a house, go straight on another wide track down through oak woods to reach a large field on the left. The track continues through rolling fields, all very pastoral and peaceful (keep on the main track), reaching a narrow road where you turn left for a couple of minutes to meet a wider road (2hrs 30 mins).

**13** Turn left following the signpost St-Romain, and shortly after bear right by the sign 'Bridle path to Gourdon 4.1km' on a raised wide track through woodland. The track goes past a modern tennis court belonging to the house, seen earlier on the outskirts of St-Romain, now over on the left. The track passes the house to reach the same intersection passed earlier where you turned right (see point 4, above) (2hrs 50 mins).

Go straight across and from here retrace your steps going upwards at first and then down (3hrs 15 mins).

**Note:** instead of going back down the sunken lane (see point 2) it is possible to stick to the road, which also arrives at the church (this takes a few minutes longer).

# The Bergerac Region (Périgord Poupre)

Dordogne from the cliffs, Mauzac (walk 18)

# WALK 17
## *Around the Trémolat Horseshoe (Cingle)*

| | |
|---|---|
| **Difficulty:** | Easy, though there is some uphill climb |
| **Time:** | 3hrs |
| **Length:** | 11.5km |
| **Map:** | Cartes IGN 1936 Série Bleue Ouest Lalinde 1:25,000. |
| | **Note:** The walk is unclear on the Série Bleue map, which has not been updated. |
| **Depart from:** | Parking du Cingle de Trémolat next to the Hotel Panoramic (shut but being renovated in 2003) |
| **Signposting:** | No signposts –yellow splashes and red/white GR splashes. **Important:** Since the original yellow splashes were made, new ones have been added not always going the same way. This can be confusing, so follow the walk instructions carefully and ignore the yellow splashes where indicated. |

Although there is a lot of road hopping and the instructions have to be followed carefully, the walker is amply rewarded with lovely elevated views of the Dordogne river as it makes a dramatic loop (called a *cingle*) through typical Périgord countryside. The walk takes you through the tranquil village of Trémolat, where the Romanesque church with its attached monastery dates back to the 11–12th centuries. It was originally built to honour the miracles of the local patron saint, St Cybard.

### How to get there (from Bergerac)
Take the D660 to Lalinde. In Lalinde go straight on the D703 signposted Sauveboeuf/Mausac. Continue for 11km till you see a narrow road right signposted La Veyssière and La Borie Neuve. Go down this road for 3.5km until you reach a T-junction where you see a parking on the left just before the Hotel Panoramic (45km from Bergerac).

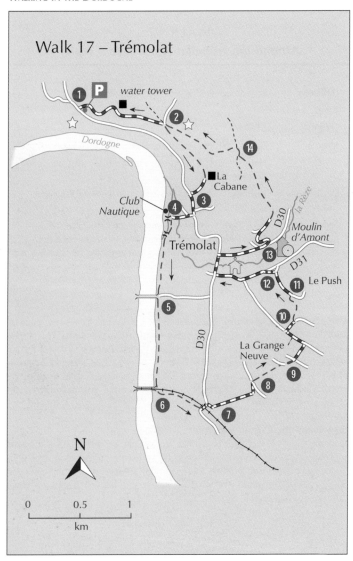

Walk 17 – Trémolat

## Directions

1. Go out of the car park and turn right and then right again following a sign Belvédère et Calvaire de Rocamadou. The narrow road goes up the hill (yellow splashes) behind the Hotel Panoramic, passing some houses to reach a water tower on the left. Just before the water tower there is a lovely view right of the Dordogne, which does a huge U-turn through cultivated fields, with low, tree-covered hills beyond.

   Continue straight on the road, descending to an intersection just after a house on the right. The GR6 comes in from the left here and goes straight ahead up a jeep track, which is where you will come in from on your return journey. Left goes to Bosredon (15 mins).

2. Turn down right immediately after the house following yellow splashes. The path is a raised track going diagonally down the hill and you catch occasional glimpses of the river below through the trees. The path turns a corner round a small white building (water pumping station) and descends through trees, past gardens and houses. The track becomes paved at a place called La Cabane and reaches a wider paved road, D30, where the yellow splashes disappear (30 mins).

*Dordogne river, Cingle de Trémolat*

**3**  Turn left, and a few minutes later turn right at a sign indicating 'Ski club de la Dordogne'. You cross a narrow stream by a bridge before coming to a barrier (entrance to the 'Club Nautique') and the main river ahead.

**4**  Turn left after the barrier and continue through a park-like area with mobile homes and spaces for caravans. **Note:** scenically it is better to keep to the edge of the river. At the end of the park you cross over a small bridge by a pond to reach a fence. Skirt round the end of the fence that is right near the water and go under the bridge on a narrow, undefined path through tall poplars and continue till it deteriorates completely (50 mins).

**5**  Turn left towards a large house to reach a jeep track where you turn right. The flat path goes through attractive fields with the Dordogne on the right (yellow splashes start here) to go under a railway bridge.

**6**  Immediately after the bridge turn left and, following yellow splashes, continue past a new water-purifying plant and orchards to reach a road where you can see the small railway station of Trémolat ahead (1hr 10 mins).

**7**  Go left across a small level crossing, and turn right to Le Rouquet and then left opposite the station. The road goes steadily upward and bends left at the top to arrive at another intersection at an old village pump and an iron cross (1hr 20 mins).
    **Note: Ignore the yellow sign just before the bend indicating a turn right off the road**.

**8**  At the old pump go straight across (yellow splashes) on a wide grassy path to reach a paved road. **Ignoring the yellow cross** turn right for 100m to reach the entrance to La Grange Neuve (1hr 30 mins).

**9**  Bear left past the pillars of La Grange Neuve (notice saying 'Private property') and continue straight. Turn left at the following T-junction. A few minutes further on turn right towards Le Rossignol. At this junction you can see on the horizon the water tower you passed at the start of the walk – it looks a long way away! You are now back on the yellow splashes.

**10**  About 100m along this road, before a sharp bend, look for a yellow splash indicating left along a grassy track (cross on post ahead). Shortly after, this track reaches a meadow. Keep left between the tall hedges. The path climbs up to a narrow tarmac road (1hr 45 mins).

*Ruins of 11th-century monastery, Trémolat*

**11** Go left (the hamlet of Le Push is to the right) along a sunken tarmac lane with old stone walls each side. It bears left downhill into a shallow valley to a T-junction, where you go left (ignore yellow arrow to the right) to reach the D31.

**12** Turn left (ignore yellow cross) into the attractive little village of Trémolat, passing new houses on the left. Turn right on the D30 towards the centre, past the Syndicat d'Initiative, which is part of a shop selling enamel souvenirs. The road crosses a pretty little stream by old houses and reaches the main square, the Romanesque church and attached former monastery. There is also a strategic bar/restaurant. *The church is worth visiting if it is open – see observations above* (2hrs).

Take the D30 behind the church, signposted St-Alvère (do not go left signposted Cingle de Trémolat), and walk out of the village.

**13** Take the second turning up left signposted Les Clidoux Haut (not the first signposted Clidoux). You can see the large building of le Moulin d'Amont further down on the right (2hrs 10 mins).

This is a steep, narrow road which goes up the side of the escarpment above the Dordogne river. The road bends to the left (steep eroded cliffs to the right) and eventually becomes a jeep track after several private houses

Boats on Dordogne nr Trémolat

– there is a shabby, round reservoir over to the left. Continue along the top of this bushy escarpment, where there are extended views.

**14** The GR6 comes in from the left, but stay on the main track, which bends to the left and continues along past a heavily fenced truffle orchard. It bends left again uphill and at the top there is a large wooden cross, from where you get glorious views of the Dordogne. From here the track descends to meet the original crossroads (see point 2, above) and a paved road. Continue straight ahead, retracing your steps past the Château d'Eau to the car park (3hrs).

**Either before or after your walk, cross the road in front of the hotel and go into a wooded picnic area for a panoramic view over the Dordogne. From here you can really appreciate the dramatic horseshoe meander of the river through rich farmland.**

# WALK 18
## *Around the Cliffs of Mauzac*

| | |
|---|---|
| **Difficulty:** | Easy, though there is a short uphill climb |
| **Time:** | 2hrs 30 mins |
| **Length:** | 9.7km |
| **Map:** | Cartes IGN Série Bleue 1936 Ouest Lalinde 1:25,000 |
| **Depart from:** | Parking in centre of Mauzac |
| **Signposting:** | Good – follow red/white splashes of the GR6, then the yellow/ red splashes which indicates a local path, followed by yellow splashes. |

Starting from the sleepy, attractive hamlet of Mauzac, right on the edge of the Dordogne river, this is a walk along wooded cliffs with magnificent views of the river as it begins a huge horseshoe meander, called the Cingle de Trémolat, through fertile flatlands with low hills on the horizon. It is a good walk to do on a hot day as most of the walking is in woodland.

Mauzac was one of the principal ports used for transporting the local Périgord wines down to Bordeaux, together with the wood used for constructing the barrels. On the return journey the boats (see explanation below) were laden with salt. Between 1838 and 1843 a canal was built to bypass La Gratusse rapids near Lalinde. These rapids were feared by the Dordogne boatmen who believed that a fearsome serpent gobbled up any boat that foundered! The dam built to supply water to the canal was heightened in 1920, and again in 1950, to feed a hydroelectric plant. This dam had repercussions on the salmon as they could not get upstream, and it was only in 1989 that a workable 'salmon passageway' was constructed.

### How to get there (from Bergerac)
Drive towards Sarlat on the D660 which follows the river. At Port de Couze, where the D660 turns right over the river, continue straight on the D703 to Lalinde. At Lalinde do not go right over the bridge to Sarlat but straight on the D703, signposted Mauzac/Le Bugue. At the end of the hamlet of Sauveboeuf 5km further on, look for a sign, right, on the narrower D31 to Mauzac 3km. Continue down to Mauzac and follow signs right to the 'Centre'. Park in the central square by the war memorial (27km east of Bergerac).

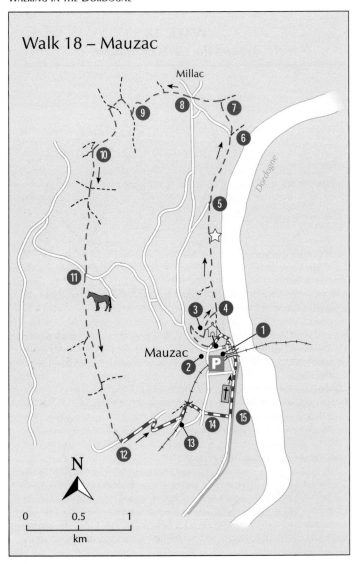

Walk 18 – Mauzac

Millac

Mauzac

Dordogne

N

0    0.5    1
km

## Directions

1   Go out of the parking and turn right and then left by a café (Le Scoop).
    Walk along with the Dordogne on the right. Shortly after turn up left where
    there are red/white splashes of the GR6 and a sign towards Au Coderc
    (name of a house) and then soon after left again following GR markings.
    You can see part of the village below and the church down on the left.

2   Bear up right at a fork a few minutes later, along a terraced hillside. You
    can see a *gariotte* (a small, round shelter of stones, which used to be used
    in medieval times by shepherds) in the woods down to the right. The path
    does a wide zigzag up to a building. Marked on the map as 'Le Théâtre
    Ruins' it has now been renovated along with a *pigonnier* (dovecot) nearby.
    There is also an orientation table overlooking the river. Here you can see
    down to the railway bridge near Mauzac and the dam for the hydroelec-
    tric installation. Further down the hill is a second *gariotte* – this one was
    strategically placed so that messages could be shouted down to the village
    below! On the side of the *pigonnier* is some ancient grafitti, discovered in
    1998. It is a primitive scratching of one of the traditional boats (called
    *gabares*) used to haul goods down river between 1770 and 1880. These
    boats, constructed in oak and beech, were 14m long, 2.7m wide and 1m
    high, and could carry 18 tons of materials such as coal or salt (15 mins).

3   Go round the building to the left and then go straight following GR splash-
    es into oak woodland. **Careful** – a few minutes later look for further GR
    splashes indicating right off the main track towards the cliff edge. Follow
    this to a T-junction (20 mins).

4   Turn left and continue along the side of the tree-covered cliff (GR sign).
    You pass a large house to the left and further on a larger, rather dilapidat-
    ed building with a ruin behind it – there are steps going down the slope
    towards the river to the right. Continue on, passing another two houses.
    Immediately after you reach an opening in the vegetation where there is
    an impressive open view of the river below as it starts its wide meander.
    You can see a small lake on the other side of the water with the ruins of
    the Moulin de Traly hidden in the trees and various small villages. On the
    horizon is a tall TV tower (40 mins). *This is an excellent perch for a picnic,
    as not only can you enjoy the view but bird lovers can watch the majestic
    flight of a pair of buzzards as they glide on the thermals hunting for food.*

5   The track joins a wide jeep track coming in from the left and you contin-
    ue on this, passing a wooden hut right called Roquebuse. The track passes
    a large field on the left with a house on a rise behind to arrive at a three-
    way intersection.

6   Take the middle track following GR splashes through fields and woodland
    to reach another fork by signposts (55 mins).

7   Turn left, signposted Pressignac (the red/white splashes of the GR go on to
    Trémolat, right). You are now following the yellow/red splashes of the GR
    du Pays (regional walk sign). Shortly afterwards you reach a road at a large
    intersection near the hamlet of Millac.

8   Go straight across two roads and, following yellow/red splashes on a tele-
    phone pole, take a wide grassy jeep track descending through woods.
    Later, where the track bends left, ignore a track coming in from the right.
    The path descends gently, traversing the wooded slope.

9   At the bottom of the valley turn sharp right and then a few minutes later
    left over a tiny stream (this could be dried up in summer). Almost imme-
    diately you come to a crossroads (crosses to left and right). Go straight up
    on a steeper, narrower track bearing left along the valley. Follow the

*Dordogne at Mauzac*

yellow/red splashes on this delightful path through widely spaced beech and oak woodland.

**10** **Careful** – at a fork go right for a few metres to reach a defined crossroads. Here you leave the yellow/red splashes, which continue straight and go left following yellow splashes. Keep to the main path. The woods become sparser and there is a low creeper-covered wall to the left. When you reach a wider stony jeep track continue straight and ignore any other paths going off, as you reach more open country and a paved road. Here the yellow/red splashes of the GR de Pays start again. **This is where the walk around Lalinde (no.19) joins until Mausac** (1hr 40 mins).

**11** Cross over the road onto a jeep track, passing a riding centre on the left and a small vineyard to reach a fork where you keep left (no splash here but crosses to right and left). Keep to the main path, descending slowly for about 20 mins through woodland and large open fields, passing a farm (Les Crozes) on the left where the road becomes paved to reach another road (2hrs).

**12** Bear left, and 5mins later turn sharp right (straight on is a cul-de-sac) and descend, passing tall fir trees with a house behind on the right and, further down, an old, partially hidden, ivy-covered *pigonnier* (dovecote). You can see a railway line ahead.

**13** Shortly after, on a hairpin bend, turn sharp left and continue along with the railway line on your right and three houses up left. A few minutes later turn off the road to the right (yellow/red splashes) and cross an arched iron footbridge over the railway to reach a road ahead.

**14** Turn left and then immediately right by an iron cross. Almost immediately turn left again on a narrower road taking you to a T-junction at the Dordogne canal (2hrs 30 mins).

**15** Turn left and walk along with the canal on the right, passing the cemetery on the left to enter Mauzac village. At the junction bear slightly right to walk back beside the river on the right, past a canal lock and the Hotel du Barrage on the left. *This is a charming little riverside hotel where you can stop and have a well-earned drink.* After going under the bridge continue to the end of the quay and turn left into the village to arrive at Le Scoop café. Go left and right to the parking area (2hrs 30 mins).

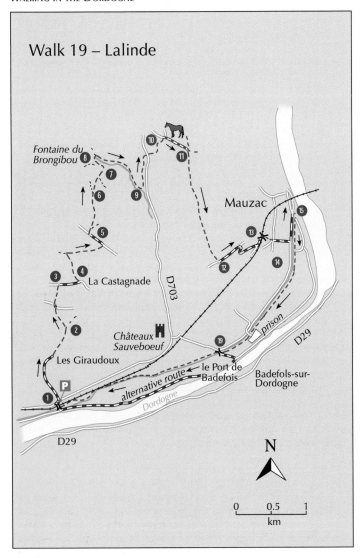

# Walk 19 – Lalinde

*Fontaine du Brongibou* 8

La Castagnade

*Châteaux Sauveboeuf*

Mauzac

prison

Les Giraudoux

le Port de Badefois

Badefols-sur-Dordogne

alternative route

Dordogne

D703

D29

D29

N

0    0.5    1
km

# WALK 19
## *A Walk around Lalinde*

| | |
|---|---|
| **Difficulty:** | Medium – a few short uphill climbs and fairly long |
| **Time:** | 4hrs |
| **Length:** | 15.2km |
| **Map:** | Cartes IGN Série Bleue 1936 Ouest Lalinde 1:25,000 |
| | **Note:** Between nos 7–10 the way has changed from the path marked on the official map |
| **Depart from:** | 1.5km from Lalinde – cross canal bridge and park on the right |
| **Signposting:** | Good – follow the red/yellow splashes of the GR de Pays and then the red/white splashes of the GR6 |

A pleasant walk in the woods and open country on the heights east of Lalinde. It includes a descent to the outskirts of the hamlet of Mausac on the Dordogne and then a walk back along the side of the canal for 5km. You get good views of the notorious La Gratusse rapids if you walk back the alternative way (see walk no.18).

The small, lively town of Lalinde was a royal English *bastide* founded by Henry III in 1267. The busy road along the Dordogne crosses to the other side of the river here towards Sarlat, so in the high season it is often clogged up with cars. It has, however, still maintained its original grid streets, market place and ancient gateway.

### How to get there (from Bergerac)
Take the direction Sarlat on the D660 which follows the river to Lalinde. At Lalinde do not go right over the bridge to Sarlat but straight on the D703 signposted Sauveboeuf/Mausac. After 1.5km cross the canal bridge and park on the right.

### Directions

1   Turn right out of the parking and cross over the railway. Take the second turning left, signposted Les Giraudoux, where there is a yellow/red splash on a telephone pole. This is a narrow paved road going medium steep upwards towards woodland. There is a house immediately right and then houses further up on the left and a high bank to the right. You reach the

large ramshackle farm of Les Giraudoux. Here the paved road becomes a grassy track, skirting a wood to reach a defined T-junction (20 mins).

2 Go left on a more defined jeep track, entering woods to reach a road a few minutes later at a corner where there are scattered houses. Go left and then straight on a track (the road bends left) into further woodland; shortly after the track meets another road (30 mins).

3 Go right, going gently downwards to reach La Castagnade, consisting of a couple of houses and a number of yappy dogs!

4 **Careful** – turn left on a narrow grassy path after a house, left, and before a walnut orchard. Continue through open fields and then into woodland, where there is a crumbling wall to the left, to reach a T-junction with a wide field and pylons in front (40 mins).

Turn right and continue down the track through attractive open fields (*lots of pyramid orchids here in springtime*) and in and out of woodland to reach another road (50 mins).

5 Turn left along the road for 400m, past a *décharge* (rubbish disposal area) and a reservoir. Look for the red/yellow splashes indicating right just after a pylon. Shortly after at a fork go left (there is a barbed-wire fence here and a sign saying 'danger'). You are now walking through continuous woodland – *the author saw a lots of white helleborine here in May*. Keep on the main path and ignore any paths coming in (usually marked with a yellow/red cross).

6 At a fork in the woods go right (careful, as this is indicated on a tree about 50m before the fork but not actually at the fork itself). Shortly after, still in woodland, you arrive at a crossroads (1hr 10 mins).

7 Go left on a track (yellow/red splashes) which curls right and then left going downwards into a shallow valley to reach a T-junction and a number of signposts.

8 Go down right following sign to La Fontaine (left is a blue dotted track going to Lalinde 13km). You reach the bottom of this valley at a delightful little picnic area with a table and benches. A sign explains that the Fontaine du Brongibou is derived from a word in the old Occitan language, 'grondement', meaning gurgling, probably an allusion to the

noise of the water. The notice also states that you are in the Foulissards, which consists mainly of oaks, where truffles can be found. *This is an idyllic, pretty spot – the stream water comes through a small arch into a 'lavoir' (large washing area) and then tumbles over into a rectangular walled pond fringed with irises which have attractive yellow flowers in May. This is the perfect spot for a picnic on a hot day.* Go over the narrow stream beyond by an arched stone bridge to reach a T-junction.

Bear right by a wooden sign following the red/yellow splashes (ignore yellow splashes to the left). You continue through this delightful wood where the trees are not too close together and the sunshine filters through. On the right beyond the vegetation there is a swampy area and another small stretch of water surrounded by tall irises and bushes. You reach a fork (1hr 30 mins).

**9** Bear up left on a narrow path with the stream alongside on the right. You can see the D703 further over. The path bears right, over the stream, to reach the road.

Go straight across the road (splashes on the asphalt) and up an ancient mule track flanked by tumbledown mossy walls to reach the hamlet of Dautres (1hr 50 mins).

**10** Turn right (ignore a road coming in from the left), passing the new house seen from the track – *this is a horse breeding area and there are numerous fields of very elegant horses*. Continue on the road until it crosses a jeep track (**here the walk descriptive joins point 11 of the walk round the cliffs of Mausac**).

*Marketplace in Lalinde*

**11** Turn right on the jeep track (the red/white splashes are not very evident here), passing a riding centre on the left and a small vineyard to reach a fork where you keep left (no splash here, but crosses to right and left). Keep to the main path, descending slowly for about 20 mins through woodland and large open fields, passing a farm (Les Crozes) on the left where the track becomes paved to reach another road (2hrs 15 mins).

**12** Bear left and then 5mins later turn sharp right (straight on is a cul-de-sac) and descend, passing tall fir trees with a house behind on the right and further down a *pigonnier* (dovecote). You can see the railway line ahead.

**13** Shortly after, on a hairpin bend, turn sharp left and continue along with the railway line on the right and three houses up left. A few minutes later turn off the road to the right (yellow/red splashes) and cross an arched iron footbridge over the railway to reach a road ahead (2hrs 30 mins).

**14** Turn left and then right by a cross. Almost immediately turn left again on a narrower road taking you to a T-junction at the Dordogne canal. Turn left and walk along with the canal on the right, passing a cemetery on the left to reach a junction at the entrance to Mausac village (2hrs 45 mins). *If you wish to have a look at Mausac village, continue straight past the lock and down a narrow road beside the river on the right. There is a pleasant little hotel here where you can get refreshments.*

**15** **Note: you have now joined the GR6 coming in from Mausac.** At the junction turn right over the lock and then right again, passing the dam on the river, left (electricity), on a flat, narrow road along the other side of the canal. Just after the dam at a fork turn right (left goes to Loubats). After the last house the paved road turns into a jeep track. *The canal is bordered by poplar, aspen and acacia trees; the white blooms of the latter are very*

### Alternative return

Turn down left on a narrow road and then turn right at the bottom and walk along the tarmac road beside the river towards the bridge where you have left your car. You get lovely views of the river as it rushes over flat rocks and swirls around tiny islands (the infamous La Gratusse rapids) and past the village of Badefois-sur-Dordogne on the opposite bank (2.9km).

*The village of Badefols-sur-Dordogne*

*attractive during the month of May. The canal itself is unused, so it is overgrown and bushy – it is navigable only beyond Lalinde.*

The path passes the tall security fences of the Mausac Detention Centre which is on both sides of the water. By the main entrance there is a bridge over the canal to the right – here you catch a glimpse of the Dordogne which is never far off on the left. The jeep track has become paved again (3hrs 15 mins). The path continues and after about 10 mins reaches the Port of Badefois, which was an important staging post for the boats transporting goods up the canal before the roads were built. Now the warehouses have been tastefully renovated into private houses.

**16** Cross the bridge over the canal at the Port (white/red GR splashes) and continue along a grassy path with the canal now on the left. There are houses from time to time on the right and a football field. Further over on the right are the turreted roofs of the Château de Sauveboeuf. Continue on the path which is straight and flat (there is a large *village de vacances* on the other side of the canal) until you reach the bridge where you parked the car (4hrs).

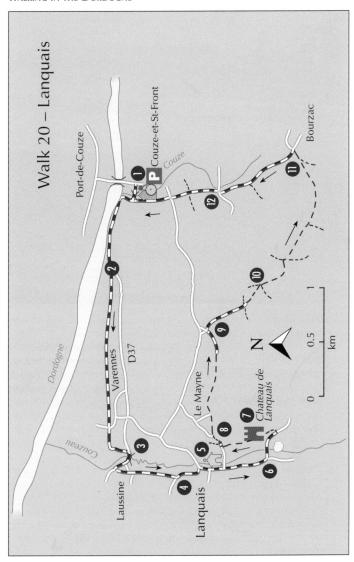

Walk 20 – Lanquais

# WALK 20
## *Couze to the Château of Lanquais*

| | |
|---|---|
| **Difficulty:** | None – mostly flat |
| **Time:** | 2hrs 30 mins plus time to look round the Château Lanquais (about 45 mins). The visit to the Paper Museum (free) takes about 20 mins. |
| | **Note:** The château is closed on Tuesdays. |
| **Length:** | 10.9km |
| **Map:** | Cartes IGN Série Bleue 1836 Est Creysse 1:25,000. A small part of the walk is on 1837 Est Castillonnès. |
| **Depart from:** | Parking area by the Paper Mill Museum (La Rouzique) |
| **Signposting:** | No splashes at all until halfway round the walk – then the white/red splashes of the GR6 followed by the yellow/red of a local walk. |

An interesting walk, though much of it on minor roads – a view of the Dordogne, the mills of Couze (local river), a Romanesque church and the famous Château de Lanquais.

On the banks of the Couze river are the vestiges of a dozen paper mills, some dating back to the 15th century. Their silent tall chimneys are a reminder that until the 19th century this area was famous for paper making. One of the mills (Moulin de Couze-la-Rouzique) was restored in 1991 and now houses an interesting museum with a rare collection of watermarks and paper-making machinery. They are once again producing watermarked paper using the traditional methods. The museum is open April to mid-October 9.30–12.30 and 14.30 to 18.30.

The Château de Lanquais was originally constructed in the 15th century but was partially destroyed by the English in the Hundred Years' War. During the 16th century, its Catholic owner Isabeau de Limeuil decided to have it restored in the style of the Louvre in Paris. Unfortunately, before it was finished the Protestant armies laid seige to the château so that the work was never completed. As you stand in front of the imposing building you can see where the Renaissance wing was added on the left-hand side with its dormer windows and ornamentation contrasting with the towers and massive chimneys of the original medieval architecture. Behind the château is an enormous 16th-century *grange* (barn) which now holds music concerts. See below for château visiting times.

## How to get there (from Bergerac)

Take the D660, direction Sarlat, along the side of the Dordogne through Creysse, Mouleydier, Tuilières and St-Capraise-de-Lalinde to Port de Couze. At Port de Couze cross the river and take the second small turning right signposted Varennes/Lanquais and Musée (19km from Bergerac). After 100m park your car to the left in front of the Moulin de Couze-la-Rouzique (see explanation above) – you can see the mill stream and a small weir with cliffs beyond.

## Directions

1  Go out of the car park and turn left on a bridge over the River Couze. Then turn right on the Route de Varennes (ignore red/yellow splashes to left; this is the way you will return). The D37 road goes by two large, tall brick chimneys on the right as it curls round to the left and the Dordogne appears on the right. The road bears away from the river passing a water purifying station.

2  A few minutes later take a narrower road down right off the D37 (15 mins) and continue along this flat, straight road with fields on the right and a high bushy bank on the left, passing a *source* (spring) coming out from a rock face above a small stagnant pool. You can see the backs of the houses of Varennes village up on the left. Do not continue round to the left to Varennes and the D37 but take a lesser road ahead, which bends to the left and reaches a T-junction (35 mins).

3  Go right and cross the Couzeau on a bridge to continue up to the hamlet of Laussine. Take the second road left, signposted Laussine, by a small iron cross. After some fields, pass a delightful small château on the left (Château Laroque) to arrive at a T-junction on the D37.

4  Go left on the road, which curls right and then left, passing the wall of the cemetery to yet another T-junction (55 mins).

5  Turn right into the village of Lanquais passing a Romanesque church with 14th-century doors (it is worth taking a few minutes to look round the church if it is open). There is a large iron cross near the church dating from the 11th century. *Lanquais is a typical Périgord village with some lovely old*

*houses, an attractive square and a covered market place.* Continue along the main street.

6    After leaving the village, take the second road to the left signposted to the château, just before a small artificial lake, which is the site of a holiday centre (*centre de loisirs*). Go over a small old bridge and continue upwards

Medieval side of
Château de Lanquais

### Château de Lanquais

The Château de Lanquais is worth visiting. The rooms are furnished in the style of the 15th and 16th centuries, the most interesting features being the enormous ornate fireplaces in sculptured stone, the dining room laid out for a typical meal (there is even a 17th-century menu where you can see they ate well) and the different utensils in the two kitchens (one Renaissance, the other medieval).

**Opening times:** December/January/February by appointment only. March/April/October/November 14.30–18.30. May/June/September 10.30–12.30 and 14.30–18.30. Shut on Tuesdays. July and August 10 – 19.00 every day. Tel. 0553.612424.

till you see a sign, left, which takes you on a rough track to the main gates of the château. Take a good look at the front of the château to appreciate the different styles of architecture – Renaissance to the left, medieval to the right (1hr 20 mins).

7   Go round the back of the château either way down past a huge medieval barn or *grange* on the left with its impressive sloping roof to reach a road by a wooden cross where you turn right, joining the GR6.

8   After 30m bear up right on a grassy track (red/white splashes), and immediately after take the first turning left (splashes on tree) out of the bushes into a field. The track climbs the hill, bearing round left at the top in front of a farm (Le Mayne on the map). *Look back and you get a good view of Lanquais behind in a shallow valley.*

   Do not take the road which goes past a house but head up right on a narrow path where there is a red/white GR sign, through fields of marguerites (large white daisies) in springtime. Cross a jeep track and continue straight through woodland and fields. Then the path starts to go downwards where there are houses over on the left. Keep going, and after a vineyard on the right the way becomes paved to reach a small crossroads.

9   Turn right following red/white GR splashes and red/yellow splashes and go down a road with some very nice houses. After 5 mins it deteriorates into a jeep track. Continue on the main track to another T-junction where there is a farm ahead (1hr 50 mins).

**10**  Turn right and continue on the track which curves left to reach another T-junction where you turn right (the GR splashes go off left) and then almost immediately left following red/yellow splashes. The track continues through small fields surrounded by hedges and in and out of woodland – keep straight on the wide jeep track going gently down and ignore any paths going off. The track reaches a house left and becomes paved before coming to a small crossroads (2hrs 05 mins).

**11**  Turn left on a road going past a number of houses – note that you are leaving the red/yellow splashes at this turning so ignore the cross saying do not go this way. Continue on this road until you come to a T-junction.

**12**  Turn right, briefly rejoining the GR from the left, and then after 100m turn left at a cross on the Allées des Noyers, leaving the GR again. You are now following the red/yellow splashes of the GR du Pays and there is a metal signpost. The road passes the gaping holes of caves on the right. Do not explore them, as there have been rock falls. *These caves are the result of centuries of quarrying as the rock has been taken for building the local castles and surrounding villages.* Further on there is a football field on the right and then you come to a crossroads where you go straight – there is a good view up right of the village of Couze-et-St-Front.

You are now entering the old part of Couze, with the little river on the right, and there are houses (uninhabited) built into the overhanging cliffs, left. You come to the old mill with its wooden mill wheel, which is now a Paper Museum. After the museum turn right on the bridge to arrive back at the car park (2hrs 30 mins).

*Moulin de Couze-la-Rouzique, Couze*

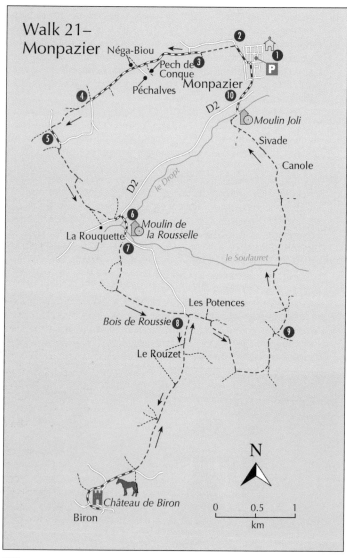

Walk 21–
Monpazier

Néga-Biou

Pech de
Conque

Péchalves

Monpazier

D2

Moulin Joli

Sivade

Canole

le Dropt

D2

Moulin de
la Rousselle

La Rouquette

le Soulauret

Les Potences

Bois de Roussie

Le Rouzet

N

Château de Biron

Biron

0    0.5    1
km

# WALK 21
## *Around Monpazier and the Château de Biron*

| | |
|---|---|
| **Difficulty:** | Easy/medium – this walk is quite long if you go all the way to the Château de Biron, but it can be shortened |
| **Time:** | 3hrs 15 mins or 4hrs 45 mins (walking to the château) |
| **Length:** | 12km or 18km |
| **Maps:** | Cartes IGN Série Bleue 1937 Ouest Beaumont, 1937 Est Belvès East and 1938 Ouest Monflanquin, which is the last section to the Château de Biron (not really necessary). Note that many of the paths do not appear on the maps, especially from points 8 to 9. |
| **Depart from:** | Central square in Monpazier |
| **Signposting:** | Good – follow the red/white splashes of the GR6 and then yellow splashes from the turning at Les Potences |

A walk around the lovely medieval village of Monpazier – it is longer by around 5km if you go to the château and back on the same path, which is rather monotonous, though the château itself, perched on top of a hill, is worth visiting. Those who don't want to walk so far can visit the château by car after the walk.

Monpazier is one of the prettiest fortified *bastide* towns in the area. Founded by the English king Edward I to establish a link between the Agen and Périgord regions, it subsequently suffered during the Hundred Years' War, being constantly pillaged and under siege, going backwards and forwards under English and then French jurisdiction. To add to their misery the citizens were plagued by a series of epidemics culminating in the dreaded Black Death. Despite all this Monpazier survived intact to the joy of countless modern visitors who now stroll through the perpendicular streets that divide the town up like a chessboard. When the town was constructed all the houses had to be built the same size with the same width of facade giving onto the street. Between each parcel of land was an open space acting as a firebreak and also used as a convenient rubbish dump! There is a beautiful main square with a wooden covered market place dating from the 16th century – look for the original grain-measuring devices which are still there. The church of St Dominic was started in the 13th century but has had many alterations over the centuries. It is worth a

173

*Square and covered market, Monpazier*

visit and has some attractive stained-glass windows. **Note:** the Tourist Bureau issues a leaflet in English of the main attractions.

Perched on a hill the majestic Château de Biron can be seen for miles around. Because of its dominant position, with the quaint village of Biron nestling at its feet, the château has been used as the site for a number of famous films including *Joan of Arc*. Built in the 11th century, the castle was acquired by Gaston de Gontaut, chief of the four Barons of Périgord. Severely damaged by the onslaught of Simon de Montfort in the 12th century it nevertheless remained in the hands of the Gontaut family for 14 generations, from the 12th to the 20th century. During the Hundred Years' War the presiding lord cleverly allied himself to the King of England or the French crown, depending on who was winning at the time, and the château escaped being ransacked. Each succeeding lord altered and restructured the château according to his whim, most of the works being done between the 15th and 17th centuries, to bequeath to posterity the impressive monument we see today.

## How to get there from Bergerac

Take the D660, direction Sarlat, for 19km. At Port-de-Couze turn right over the Dordogne and continue on the D660 for another 26km, through Beaumont to Monpazier. Go into the centre and park in one of the many parking areas – parking could be difficult in the high season as this is one of the most attractive villages in France and busy with tourists. Make your way to the central square.

## Directions

1    In the main square looking across towards the magnificent wooden covered market (Halle-aux-Grains), turn immediately right (west) into the Rue Porte-Compan by a café/tabac with a PMU sign. Go down, crossing the Rue St-Pierre where you see your first red/white GR36 splash. A few metres further on turn right and then left into the Routes des Squayres. Continue down the road for about 300m (5 mins).

2    Turn left on a jeep track that goes down then upwards (medium steep) becoming paved again at a large house on the left that has a beautiful view of Monpazier on the opposite hill. *In May, while photographing a 'pigonnier' (dovecot) in a field along this jeep track, the author discovered a small patch of bee orchids.* Continue (ignoring a road coming in from the left) till you meet a road at a bend (15 mins).

3    Go straight on the road towards the farms of Pech de Conque, Néguebio (on the map this is Néga-Biou, a classic example of the difference between maps and signposts) and Péchalves. The road descends slightly, curving left round a delightful open, shallow valley and then up again, continuing flat passing the three entrances to the farms. At the entrance to Péchalves there is a delightful old *lavoir* (wash trough). This is high ground with extensive views and you can see the imposing Château de Biron on the horizon, left (35 mins).

**4**   As the road turns left, go straight on a narrow path (GR splashes) through woodland and fields to reach the same road again by a cross (45 mins).

**5**   Turn left and continue down to where the road bends to the left at a large dilapidated house which is being renovated and go straight on a jeep track. Shortly after, at a fork, go right (red/white splashes) through woods descending gently to a shallow valley. Keep to the main track and ignore any paths going off as you descend, passing a ruin, to the D2 road where there is a wooden cross. There is a lovely old house on the opposite side of the road called La Roquette which was once a tile factory; you can still see the two old chimneys (1hr).

**6**   Turn left and then a few minutes later turn right (signposted Gaugeac) onto a smaller road which goes by the idyllic, renovated Moulin de la Rousselle – the adjacent stream is fringed with yellow irises and has white ducks swimming on it (1hr 15 mins).

**7**   After the mill, where the road curves round to the left, look for a jeep track going up right (clear splashes). Walk up the track to reach a wooded upland area consisting of tall pines, gorse, broom, juniper and bracken. Keep on the wide jeep track through widely spaced tall woodland. It bears to the left (do not go straight ahead) and you keep to the main track through woodland (the Bois de Roussie) for around 30 mins. There is a lack of red/white GR splashes along here. Eventually you come out into wide, flat fields bordered by trees to arrive at a T-junction and a narrow paved road (there is a GR sign just before to warn you).

**8**   Turn right (there is a wooden hut nearby and piles of logs) and continue for about 50m to reach the junction called Les Potences, where you have the choice to go an extra 2.5km to the Château de Biron (see right) or continue the walk (1hr 35 mins).

    **Note: in all this is a distance of 5km there and back on a rather boring, straight, unmade road fringed with trees from which you get no views except at the very end, where there is a magnificent view of the château perched on a rise.**

    At Les Potences (if you do not go to the château) go left by a wooden cross, passing a small shuttered house, into open fields. Where the track bears left to Les Potences, which you can see on the horizon, go straight on following yellow splashes down a narrow path into chestnut woods and after 200m bearing right to arrive at a junction in the woods. **Note:**

## To continue to the château

Walk down the unpaved road going slightly downhill and then gently upwards passing a sign to the right indicating Le Rouzet and then a fence with a young plantation to the right. Ignore a large track coming in from the right and continue straight. A few minutes before the road meets a paved road there is an old house to the right which has a lovely view of the château. At the paved road turn right and, passing the old stables (beautifully renovated), make your way to the main entrance up steps from the attractive village of Biron. Here you can take refreshment at a very welcome restaurant. The château is open all year round.

**Opening times:** February–March and October–December: Tuesday–Sunday 10.00–12.30 and 14.00–17.30. April daily (times as above). May, June and September daily until 18.30. July and August daily until 19.00. Guided visits take about 45mins.

Retrace your steps back to Les Potences and follow point 8 – extra time 1hr 30 mins.

*Château de Biron, near Monpazier*

**Follow the yellow splashes carefully as these paths are not shown on the map due to extensive logging.** Go left and then immediately left again at a fork. The track continues to reach the edge of the woods at a field (there is a yellow splash on a large chestnut tree). Bear right skirting the field. **Careful** – take a narrow turning right off the main track and continue along through chestnut forest interlaced with tall pines, crossing straight over two small crossroads to reach a jeep track.

Turn left on the jeep track and continue to reach a large crossroads in the woods.

9 **Careful** – take the second and narrower path right between two pines and at a fork keep right (yellow splashes). This is a narrow, bushy path flanked by broom and juniper that descends gently into a shallow valley through attractive, widely spaced woodland, where there are some magnificent old chestnut trees, and crosses small clearings. Keep going on a wider track which joins from the left.

Keep going following yellow splashes. At a fork keep left and go down a sunken path to cross a little stream called Le Soulauret (2hrs 34 mins). *Apparently the water in this stream never goes above 4 degrees no matter what time of year it is!* The path climbs upwards and then undulates along, coming out of the woods at a large open field to the left, and then goes back into woods again a few minutes later. At a fork keep down to the right (2hrs 45 mins).

The path continues on, briefly going into the woods again and then skirting them on a narrow overgrown path with large open fields on the left – you pass the large farms of Canole and Sivade, with its tobacco drying shed, on the horizon up right. You can now see the village of Monpazier ahead. The path goes into a sort of mini-ravine which was caused by a violent storm in 1917 and then continues down and bears right over a small wooden bridge over the Dropt stream to reach an old mill (le Moulin Joli) which used to process nuts into oil. Pass the mill to reach the road (3hrs).

10 Cross the D2 road and go steeply up another road leading to the Gateway St Jacques and the entrance to Monpazier (3hrs 15 mins).

# WALK 22
## *Around the Fortified Village of Beaumont*

| | |
|---|---|
| **Difficulty:** | An easy walk in the countryside around Beaumont – three ascents and descents into shallow valleys |
| **Time:** | 3hrs 30 mins plus time to look at the church and fortified village of Beaumont |
| **Length:** | 13.8km |
| **Map:** | Cartes IGN Série Bleue 1937 Ouest Beaumont (Dordogne) 1:25,000 |
| **Depart from:** | Parking by the church in the centre of Beaumont |
| **Signposting:** | No signposts but excellent yellow splashes round the walk – follow yellow walk no.2 |

A delightful walk through pastoral countryside – wide sweeping fields of crops and walnut orchards but few vineyards. Some walking through woodland and in and out of shallow valleys.

Beaumont, one of the renowned *bastide* towns of this area (see Introduction), was founded in 1272 by Lucas de Thanay, a lieutenant of the English King Edward I. The streets were laid out in the form of an H and, although much of the original design has disappeared, it still retains an air of neatness as the streets intersect at right angles round a main square. All that remains of the impressive ramparts is the Porte de Luzier, which you go through at the start of the walk. The huge, rather grim, 13th-century fortified church dominates the square with its four big towers and windowless walls – the only graceful feature being an elegant Gothic doorway with a finely carved balustrade above.

### How to get there (from Bergerac)
Take the D660 from Bergerac crossing the Dordogne at the Port de Couze and continuing all the way to Beaumont (30km). Follow all directions to the centre of Beaumont and park in the parking opposite the church.

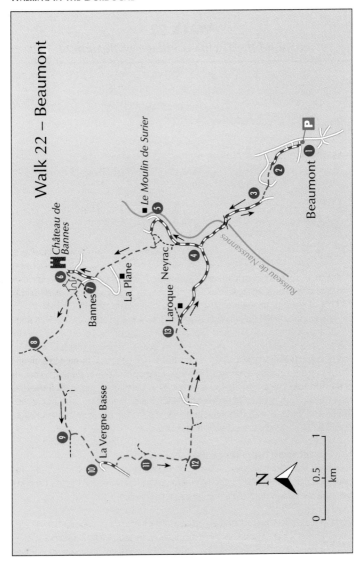

Walk 22 – Beaumont

## Directions

1  From the central square follow the sign 'Porte de Luzier' down some steps towards the walls surrounding the village and turn right immediately on the Rue Feliciane. At the end by a small tower go straight across. At the next intersection continue straight on the Rue de la Tour de Banne which goes down passing a squat stone building (water source) on the right to reach a wider road at a T-junction (10 mins).

2  Just before the T-junction go left and immediately straight down a wide, grassy path. About 20m before you reach another road go right down a narrower path into a cobbled tunnel going underneath the road and then down into a shallow valley (farms on right) to reach yet another road.

3  Turn right and continue along, crossing over the Naussannes stream by a bridge and turn right, direction Surier-Bannes.

4  At a fork go right in the direction of Neyrac (left goes to Laroque, and this is where you will come out towards the end of the walk). The road goes gently upwards, and the shallow valley is down on the right with the stream coursing through it. Further on keep to the road proper and do not take the sign up left to Neyrac. Now you can see, below right, a large pond and small chalets of a new camping area called Le Moulin de Surier (40 mins).

5  Walk past the chalets, and just before the main entrance turn up left, direction La Crouzille, on a narrow road going upwards, and then at a corner just before a private house turn left again onto a grassy track through a wood (yellow splashes not obvious). Ignore two paths coming in from the left and then keep right on the main stony track at a corner (big farm over on the left). Continue up past fields and woods to arrive at an intersection by a large farm called La Plane on the left. **Careful** (yellow splash again not obvious) – continue straight downwards along a narrow grassy track with hedges either side to arrive at a crossroads. The road ahead goes to the Eglise de Bannes but turn right for 200m, where you get your first view of the turrets of the Château de Bannes (1hr 15 mins).

6  Turn up left in front of the château (yellow splashes) ignoring the private property sign. Just before the main gates head back sharp left onto a grassy lane. *This attractive château, built in the 15th century, sits on a crag*

*Porte de Luzier, Beaumont*

*overlooking the Couze valley. It is now in private hands and being renovated.* Walk up the lane and after a few minutes look for steps to the right which lead to the lovely Romanesque church of St Martin near the hamlet of Bannes. *Here is an extended view over the wood-covered valley of La Couze. It is worth taking a look into the church, which has a grill over the entrance but is open. It dates from the 12th century and was built on an ancient religious site. It was renovated in the 18th century and more recently in 1993.* Continue on the pathway in front of the church to an old stone cross in the hamlet, which seems to consist of only a couple of houses (1hr 15 mins).

7   Turn right on a jeep track and then right again down a grassy track, descending gently into La Couze valley for 1.2km. Keep right at an early fork and follow the yellow splashes carefully as you go along with the stream flowing on the right. At the bottom of the valley are a number of tall poplar trees and a T-junction where there are yellow splashes right and left.

8   Turn left following yellow splash 2 to go along another shallow valley called a combe. There is a large field at the bottom and woods on the low slope beyond. Avoid any turnings off which are clearly marked with a cross. The track goes by overhanging cliffs to the right (you can see the hooks of climbers in the cliff wall) and if you look carefully this cliff continues near the path in the trees for a while.

9   Ignore a left turn at the start of an ivy-covered wall but take the next turn 80m further on (1hr 45 mins). The path rises gently out of the combe, with a high wall on the right and then bordered by low, mossy stone walls (probably an ancient mule track) to reach the hamlet of La Vergne Basse and a paved road (2hrs).

10  Continue on the road straight through the hamlet and then turn left between two houses (yellow marks) and continue down into another wooded, shallow valley.

11  At an intersection at the bottom do not turn left (marked 'lavoir') but go right following yellow splashes carefully through the woods. Continue upwards out of the valley and along the side of the hill to reach a T-junction (2hrs 30 mins).

12  Turn left on a path undulating along by young walnut orchards and through open fields where you have extended views. Keep to the wide jeep track and ignore any paths coming in (clearly marked with a cross). Go straight across a paved road onto a jeep track, passing a walnut orchard to the right and descending gently to reach a crossroads at the fortified manor of Laroque, which is off to the left (3hrs).

13  Here the jeep track becomes a paved road, which you continue on as it goes up and down through mainly open country till you reach the fork described at point 4 (see above). Turn right and retrace your steps to Beaumont as per the outward journey (3hrs 30 mins).

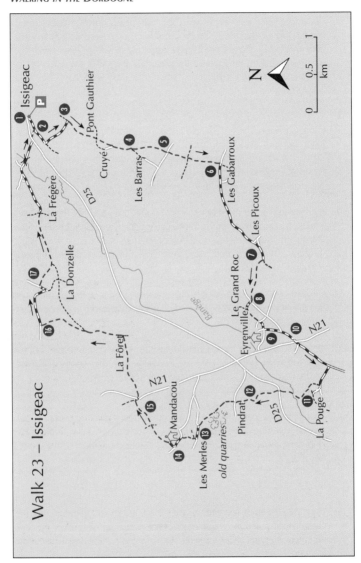

Walk 23 – Issigeac

# WALK 23
## *Around the Medieval Village of Issigeac*

| | |
|---|---|
| **Difficulty:** | An easy but long country walk through the rolling fields and woods around Issigeac |
| **Time:** | 4hrs plus time to stroll around the medieval village |
| **Length:** | 16.3km (it says 15.5km on the map in the square and 16km on the wooden signpost alongside!) |
| **Map:** | Cartes IGN Série Bleue 1837 Est Castillonnès 1:25,000 |
| **Depart from:** | Square with covered market in front of information map |
| **Signposting:** | Good – one or two signposts but otherwise yellow splashes or wooden posts with yellow splashes. For some of the time you are on the red/white splashes of the GR636. |

A delightful walk through lanes bordered by cow parsley, in and out of woodland, up and down small, dank dells and shallow valleys, through wide fields of cereals where you can see the rolling, beautiful countryside stretching into infinity, hidden hamlets and tastefully restored expensive-looking houses. To cap it all there is a stroll round the *bastide* medieval village of Issigeac, which has changed little since the 15th century, when it was a prosperous community and the *bourgeois* built their half-timbered houses with sculptures and decorated faces (*maison des têtes*). There is a lively street market on Sunday mornings.

### How to get there (from Bergerac)
Take the N21 from Bergerac and then turn left on the D14, signposted Issigeac. At the entrance to the village turn right, direction Eymet, and park in the square where there is a covered *halle* (covered market); post office and information map (22km from Bergerac).

### Directions

1    Take a look at the information map first, to the right at the entrance to the square, and you will see exactly where you are going. Follow the sign 'Boucle d'Issigeac' down a narrow road going out of the village past some majestic chestnut trees.

2    At the first intersection turn left (on the right is the leafy lane with a 'No entrance' sign where you will emerge on your return), and go through open fields for 200m (yellow post). Keep on the road as it bends to the left by a house (do not go straight on a grassy path) passing a *pigonnier* (dovecote) with a house attached to it to arrive at another intersection (yellow post).

3    Take the second right (not immediate right going to a house) on a grassy path lined with hedges and continue on, passing some buildings over on the left (Pont Gauthier) and later a large farm called Cruyé. The path goes straight, descending slightly for 300m (20 mins).

4    Turn left on a jeep track (the cluster of buildings up to the right is called Les Barras). **Careful** – after a yellow post (not easy to see) take a narrow path left with a hedge right and fields on the left towards scattered woodland. The track goes by a pond and a house before reaching the road (35 mins).

5    Cross the road and continue on another jeep track ascending gently past a large house over on the right.

6    Shortly afterwards you reach another road, where you turn right and follow the road for 1.5km, passing the hamlet of Les Gabarroux to the left – you are on an open road with wide fields of crops on each side and sweeping views. The road continues past the hamlet of Les Picoux.

7    Soon afterwards go off the road to the right (1hr 5 mins) by a curious rusty crane (post). The sunken jeep track ascends for about 100m and then comes out into open fields before going into a tree-lined lane to descend towards a road and the hamlet of Le Grand Roc (1hr 20 mins).

8    Turn left and then immediately right on a jeep tracking passing the huddled buildings of Grand Roc. Bear left by a wooden crucifix down a narrow grassy track. As you walk through fields of white daisies and pyramid orchids in springtime with vineyards to the right, you can see the spire of Eyrenville church ahead. There is an iron cross to the left as you reach the road. Go past the church with a cemetery alongside into a very pretty little hamlet with some attractive houses (1hr 30 mins).

9    At the square turn left by a huge iron cross and walk out of the hamlet. A few minutes later at a further cross bear right again and walk up to the N21 road (right to Bergerac/left to Villeneuve-sur-Lot).

*Market day in Issegeac*

10  Go straight across on to the lesser C1 road, and after about 600m turn right, direction La Pouge, by a wooden sign indicating Boucle Issigeac. **Note: at this turning you have joined the red/white splashes of the GR636, so follow these as the yellow splashes temporarily disappear.** The road bends left and right.

11  **Careful** – just before houses go right (the more obvious path right has a GR cross on a tree) down a narrow, dank, bushy lane to reach the shalllow Banège valley. Cross a stream on a rather rickety bridge and pass the buildings of le Moulin de la Pouge, right. Almost immediately you ascend gently, past some houses (you feel as though you are passing through someone's garden), to reach the D25 (2hrs).

Cross over and go up a sunken lane, initially by the side of an attractive house. It climbs up quite a way passing a rocky area covered by bushes and trees (on the map is says these are ancient quarries). The path becomes a wider jeep track with pines on the left and then becomes paved as it reaches a scattering of houses at Pindrat.

12  Go right and then almost immediately left onto a jeep track (well marked red/white GR signs) – there is a lovely view here over the valley with the Route Nationale going through. The track passes more substantial tree-covered quarries. Avoid a path to the right after a ruin as the main

path bends left (well signed) and goes into woods before reaching another road at Les Merles (2hrs 15 mins).

**13** Go straight ahead on the road for about 70m, and then turn down right into a bushy, shallow valley with fields at the bottom, and then steeply up again to the church of Mandacou. Bear up left through the village. **Note: here the red/white splashes of the GR636 continue north of the village. From here follow the wooden posts with yellow marking.**

**14** In the village follow a smart wooden sign indicating 'Boucle de Issigeac' to the right down a narrow lane. Following a post with yellow splashes turn a corner onto a jeep track and continue down this bushy track (do not go down right after the house). Continue onwards with a hedge on the left and go straight at a grassy intersection with the hedge on the right. The track then goes gently downwards on a leafy lane, past a tumbledown shack up in the woods, left, with a final wiggle to the right to reach the N21 again (2hrs 40 mins).

**15** Cross over the road and follow the sign 'Le Mayne'. Continue on this flat jeep track (large building up to the right). Go straight when the jeep track curls to a house (La Fôret) on the left (yellow post) and go through woods to the brow of the hill, where the path curls left to reach a wide plateau where there are sweeping views. The track cuts through delightful open country and scattered woodland (*we were lucky enough to see a field full of large lady orchids in early May*). After going gently right and left you can see a large estate (La Donzelle) up to the right. Continue to meet another road (3hrs 15 mins).

**16** Go right along the road for about 800m and then left, direction Monsaguel, just before La Donzelle (yellow posts).

**17** About 150m further on turn right onto a jeep track and follow yellow signs round to the left heading slightly uphill, keeping to the main path, passing a renovated house on the left (La Grande Borie). At the entrance to the house the track becomes stony and then paved as it reaches a scattering of houses at La Frégère. Continue on the winding road for about 1km, ignoring signs left to La Vernelle and La Loge-du-Pévot. Cross a river on a bridge with a poplar wood to the left to reach a T-junction at the D25. Turn left for a few metres and go up right on a narrow lane (yellow post) to reach the fork at point 2 (see above). Continue to the information panel (4hrs).

# WALK 24
## Conne-de-Labarde

| | |
|---|---|
| **Difficulty:** | Easy, undulating walk |
| **Time:** | 2hrs 45 mins |
| **Length:** | 10.6km |
| **Map:** | Cartes IGN Série Bleue 1837 Est Castillonnès |
| **Depart from:** | In front of the Salle des Fêtes, Conne-de-Labarde |
| **Signposting:** | Some red/white splashes of the GR6 where applicable – otherwise no splashes or signposting |

Apart from some road walking which includes 1km along a fairly major road (for this part of the world), it is a pleasant undulating walk through fields, vineyards and woodland in unspoilt countryside. Conne-de-Labarde is a small hamlet with a pretty Romanesque church dominated by a high wall containing three bells (*clochers-murs*), a style of architecture typical of the region.

**How to get there (from Bergerac)**
Take the N21 for 8km and then look for a sign to the left indicating Conne-de-Labarde 3km. Go left and then park in front of the Salle des Fêtes at the entrance to the hamlet.

**Directions**

1   With the Salle des Fêtes behind you go down the road in the direction of St-Aubin-de-Lanquais passing the old *lavoir* (washing area) on the right, then the church and finally a large, messy farm as you walk out of the hamlet. Follow the red/white GR splashes as the road goes gently downwards to reach a T-junction by an attractive pond fringed with lovely yellow irises in springtime (10 mins).

2   Turn left, still following the red/white GR splashes. The road bends gently right as you enter the shallow Conne valley. Keep on the road (ignore grassy turning left) to reach the pretty Moulin de Lestrade, which has been

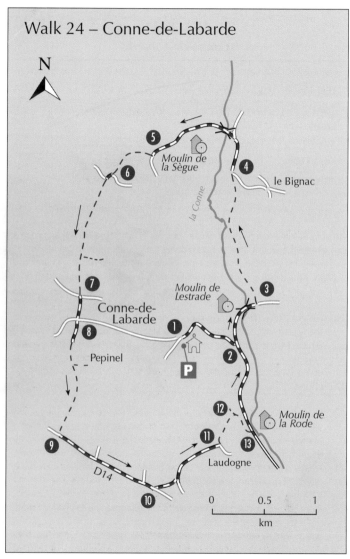

Walk 24 – Conne-de-Labarde

N

Moulin de la Sègue

le Bignac

la Conne

Moulin de Lestrade

Conne-de-Labarde

Pepinel

P

Moulin de la Rode

Laudogne

D14

| 0 | 0.5 | 1 |

km

tastefully renovated. You can see the millstream, and across the road is a small pond (15 mins).

3    After crossing the stream twice take the first turning to the left, following the GR, on a jeep track which eventually deteriorates into a path. You are walking along the side of the valley; to the left are fields of crops traversed by the Conne stream and to the right is woodland. Later on you can see the buildings of Le Bignac up on the right, and the path reaches a road at a T-junction (35 mins).

4    Turn left on the road (ignore the red/white GR splashes indicating up right to the hamlet of Bignac) which veers left and joins another road before crossing the Conne Rau to reach le Moulin de la Sègue on the left. The road bends gently uphill to a large restored house at the top called Les Plantades by an unusual square *pigeonnier* (dovecote) (55 mins).

5    Go off right just before the *pigeonnier* onto a grassy track, keeping a vine-yard on the left, to reach a fountain on the right, Fontaine de Malamont. Continue on the path through further vineyards to meet a road at a corner.

6    Go straight on the road for about 50m and then continue straight (the road bends to the right) on a rough track. Ignore a track coming in from the right as you continue through patches of open country, woodland and the occa-sional vineyard. *We saw an attractive cluster of loose flowered orchids here in May (*Orchis laxiflora*).* If you look left you can see the high bell tower of Conne-de-Labarde church. There are no splashes or indications of any kind, but keep going on the grassy track which passes under tele-phone wires and by vineyards on the left to meet another road at a corner.

7    Go straight ahead on the road following the red/white splashes of the GR, which has come in from the left. Continue on to reach a crossroads where Conne-de-Labarde is indicated left (1hr 20 mins).

8    Go straight on towards Pepinel (the red/white splashes of the GR now go off to the right) past two new houses to the left and continue on the undefined track through open, attractive countryside of vineyards, fields and wood-land, past two adjacent ponds on the right to eventually reach the D14 road.

9    Turn left along the road for 1.5km. Ignore two small roads to the left, both going to Conne-de-Labarde – in between, also on the left, is a restored

house (château), but it is surrounded by hedges so there is little to see. Continue to another turning left, signposted Laudogne (2hrs).

10  Go left for a few minutes and then turn left again, still following the sign-post Laudogne, on a rough road past a beautiful restored house on the right which has a delightful view down the Conne valley.

11  **Careful** – at a bend to the right which leads to another large house, turn down left on a rough track into the wooded valley to reach a T-junction at the valley bottom by a stream.

12  Go right through woods to meet a rough road at houses and then further on to reach another T-junction.

13  Turn left along a straight wooded road, with the ruined Moulin de la Rode on the right hidden in the trees, to reach the original junction taken on the outward journey (point 2, above). (Here the red/white splashes of the GR start again.) Turn up left and retrace your steps to the village (2hrs 45 mins).

# WALK 25
## *Le Circuit de St-Aubin*

| | |
|---|---|
| **Difficulty:** | An easy walk with no height gain through meadows and woodland |
| **Time:** | 3hrs |
| **Length:** | 11km |
| **Map:** | Cartes IGN Série Bleue 1837 Est Castillonnès 1:25,000. **Note:** The GR6 has been rerouted since the map was published. |
| **Depart from:** | Parking beside the church at St-Aubin-de-Lanquais, 12km southeast of Bergerac. |
| **Signposting:** | Good – follow the red/white splashes of the GR6 and then yellow splashes or posts. |

A delightful walk in typical Périgord Poupre countryside – through vineyards, huge open fields of barley and winter wheat, woodlands and sleepy hamlets – you feel, and are, far from the madding crowd! This area to the south of the Dordogne river benefits from a particularly mild climate – it is warmer than the northern region and has less rainfall – nevertheless, if it has rained, parts of this walk are very boggy! St-Aubin does not have a church with the traditional *clochers-murs* (wall with bells at the top), but a tall, elegant church spire, which can be seen for miles around.

### How to get there (from Bergerac)
Take the N21, direction Castillonnès/Villeneuve-sur-Lot, and after a few kilometres bear off left on the D14E/D19 through St-Nexans to St-Aubin-de-Lanquais (12km southeast of Bergerac). Park beside the church – on the adjacent green there is a notice board with a map of the surrounding area with walks outlined. There is also a wooden notice board indicating Boucle St-Aubin 11km.

### Directions

1   Go out of the parking and turn right in front of the church to reach the traffic lights at a small crossroads. Go straight, direction Faux, for a few metres and then, following the red/white splashes of the GR6, bear left

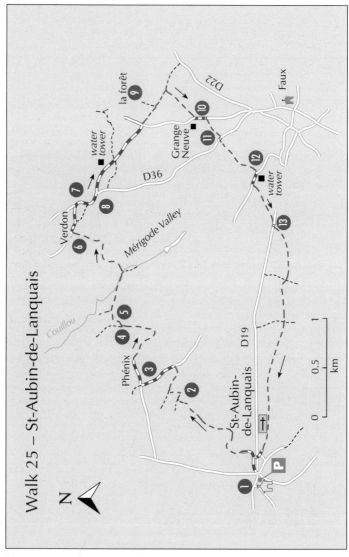

Walk 25 – St-Aubin-de-Lanquais

onto a narrow paved road which goes through a farm. Where a narrow road comes in from the right continue straight. The road bends to the left through further houses and farm buildings before becoming a grassy track. This bends to the right round a field (look for a sign on a walnut tree) and then 150m later curves to the left. The path is straight bordered by hedgerows and trees and reaches some vineyards (20 mins).

2    Continue with the hedge on your right and the vineyard on the left. In the middle of the vineyard, at a T-junction with vines in front, turn right and then left. Continue on the path curving round with a field right and vines left. At a further T-junction (field ahead) turn right. The path bears round left and you can see the village of Phénix ahead dominated by an attractive *pigonnier* (dovecot). At the paved road turn left and walk into the hamlet (30 mins).

3    In Phénix turn right at the T-junction (post box here) and continue on the paved road to a small plateau where there are lovely views in all directions, including a water tower ahead on the horizon. The road deteriorates into a wide jeep track. Keep to the main track as it descends, bending right and then left, into the shallow, tree-covered Mérigode valley.

4    Bear right at fork and continue down (50 mins).

5    At a further fork turn right in the wood and continue on with a stream on the left and a field through the trees, crossing the stream at the bottom of the valley. The track goes straight uphill by a large field on the left. *This is a magical field dotted with fir trees and a carpet of white daisies. The author has also seen bee, lady, pyramid and tongue orchids here in May.* At the top you go back into woodland, bearing left and crossing a stream again. This is a narrow, sunken path going medium-steep out of the valley to reach a minor road, where you suddenly have a panorama of fields and woods stretching to the horizon (1hr 20 mins).

6    Turn right into the hamlet of Verdon, which has a church and cemetery in the centre but little else. Contine straight to reach the D36, admiring the beautiful cottage garden on the left just before you get to the road.

7    Turn right and continue past a school on the left. There are lovely extended views of fields and woods in all directions.

*Pigonnier in Phénix*

**8** Just after leaving the sign marking the end of the village bear left (signposted La Forêt) towards a water tower you can see ahead. Continue on the narrow, flat tarmac road past the water tower to the left and ignore a path going off left with a GR cross (this is where the GR used to go, but the path has been diverted) to reach a crossroads (1hr 40 mins).

**9** Go straight on to a jeep track, well marked with posts with yellow splashes and red/white GR signs (ignoring a road going to a house on the left), and about 250m further on look for a path to the right (posts with yellow splashes and GR splashes). Walk alongside a fence to reach the road again by a large house (La Grange Neuve) and an iron cross (1hr 50 mins).

**10** Turn left and a few minutes later turn right off the road on a grassy track to reach the D36.

**11** Turn right and then immediately left (posts with yellow arrows) and continue towards the water tower at a T-junction where there is yet another glorious view – this is a good place for a picnic (2hrs 5 mins). **Note: Here you can turn left and continue towards the village of Faux, which, apart from a large church with an interesting, rather Eastern-looking tower and attractive château (private) nearby, has little of interest. Return by the same road to the water tower (about 35 mins).**

*Cemetery near St Aubin*

**12**  At the water tower turn right, leaving the red/white splashes of the GR, and continue down the road. A few minutes later turn left off the road just before a private house and go down past a new oak plantation (probably planted for truffles) to reach the D19 (2hrs 15 mins).

**13**  Turn right and, shortly afterwards, left onto a grassy track. A few minutes later bear right and later on cross over a track. Continue straight ahead into a large field where you can see the steeple of the church in St-Aubin on the horizon. The track bends to the left and into woods, where you turn left again and immediately right. Walk on with a hedge on the left and field on the right to reach vineyards. Continue straight through the vineyards, passing the small walled village cemetery on the right. You reach a fork where you turn left (you can also turn right) to arrive at the traffic lights in the village and then the church where your car is parked (3hrs).

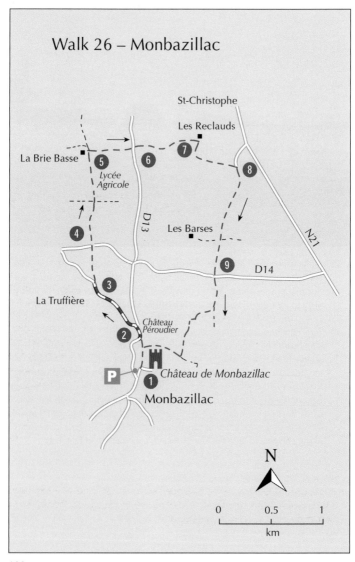

Walk 26 – Monbazillac

# WALK 26
## *Through the Vineyards of Monbazillac*

| | |
|---|---|
| **Difficulty:** | Easy, flat walk through vineyards |
| **Time:** | 1hr 45 mins plus visit to château (about 1hr – 1hr 30 mins) |
| **Length:** | 6.9km |
| **Map:** | Cartes IGN Série Bleue 1837 Ouest Eymet 1:25,000 |
| **Depart from:** | Car park for Château de Monbazillac |
| **Signposting:** | No signposts – red/white GR splashes and then no splashes, so follow explanation carefully – GR splashes start at the end again |

An easy walk through the vineyards surrounding the Château de Monbazillac. The château is set attractively on the brow of a hillside overlooking fields of the famous sweet white wine the area is renowned for. Relatively new compared to other Dordogne châteaux, it was built by François d'Aydie, Seigneur of Bergerac, in 1550. Since then it has remained exactly as it was built and never ransacked, burnt or put under siege! Owned by the Monbazillac Wine Cooperative since 1960 (you can taste and buy wines at the entrance), it is worth visiting if you have an hour to spare. The rooms have an interesting selection of antique furniture, as well as documents outlining the history of the Protestant religion, and there is a wine museum in the basement.

Open all year round except January. **Opening times:** November–March: open every day except Mondays, 10.00–12.00 and 14.00–17.00. April/May/October: open every day 10.00–12.00 and 14.00–18.00. June to September: open every day 10.00–19.00 (19.30 July/August).

### How to get there (from Bergerac)
Take the D933 south of Bergerac and then look for a sign left to Monbazillac on the D13, which crosses the D936 to continue up to the village. Park in the car park near the château (7km from Bergerac).

*Château de Monbazillac*

## Directions

**1**    Turn left out of the car park and, keeping the wall of the château on the right (if there is a chain across the road jump over it), walk down a sunken, grassy track following the red/white splashes of the GR6. Ignore a track to the right (this is where you join up at the end of the walk). Continue down to reach the D13 and the Château Péroudier on the right, a winery where you can have a *dégustation gratuite* (free tasting) of their wines.

**2**    A few metres further on turn left off the D13, signposted La Truffière. The road goes down gradually with vineyards on either side. It carries on past the buildings of the Domaine La Truffière on the left, bending to the right.

**3**    After a few minutes take a right turn off the road (indicated by splashes further up on the bend) onto a wide, grassy track. Following the red/white GR splashes on telephone poles, bear right and immediately left at a grassy intersection to walk beside the vines rather than straight down through long grass. Both ways reach a narrow paved road (20 mins).

**4**    Go straight across the road (GR crosses on both sides) and continue straight on a wide, grassy track through vineyards, crossing a jeep track leading to the buildings of the Lycée Agricole on the right and later passing a house on the left.

5   **Careful** – bear right just before a stagnant patch of water to the right and before the entrance to a smart house on the left (La Brie Basse on the map). **Note: here the GR goes straight ahead, and from now on until nearer the end of the walk there are no markings.** This is an undefined grassy path through vineyards with a ditch to the left and there are two ditches to jump across (if it has been raining and there is too much water go right along the banks where it gets narrower). The track soon reaches the D13 road again (40 mins).

6   Cross the road and go straight ahead on a lesser road, direction La Sabatière (ignore first jeep track right) to reach the buildings of the Domaine des Reclauds, where you can have another free wine tasting!

7   Turn right on a jeep track at the sign 'Domaine des Reclauds' in front of the house and continue through the vineyards where you can see the huge, turreted Château de Monbazillac on the far rise ahead. After a few minutes the track bends to the left.

8   At the second bend which would take you to the hamlet of St-Christophe, bear right on to a grassy track. Continue on this wide, sometimes unde-fined, grassy track between the vineyards with sometimes a hedge to right

*Château de Monbazillac*

Old well, Mobazillac

or left. **Always keep the château ahead of you** and ignore the track leading to the buildings of Les Barses beyond the vines over on the right. Keep to the main grassy track, bordered by wild bushes (colourful when in bloom in May) and passing plum orchards on the left before it reaches the D14 road (1hr 15 mins).

9   Cross the road and continue straight up a grassy, bushy track passing a wooden hut and a track immediately after. A few minutes later take the first obvious turning up right through a vineyard and up a bank into an orchard. Turn up left by the trees, then right at the top and then left again. Carry on the track upwards, passing a ruined building covered in creeper over on the left, and continue on where the track bends right. At the second bend right go left up the hill beside a plum orchard, right, and a ditch, left. Bear right at the top, and a few metres further on the red/white splashes of the GR6 come in from the left. Continue straight along, with the château above you on the left till you reach the original track down from the car park (point 2, above). Retrace your steps to the car park (1hr 45 mins).

# WALK 27
## *Around the Villages of Flaugeac and Singleyrac*

| | |
|---|---|
| **Difficulty:** | Easy, undulating walk |
| **Time:** | 3hrs 40 mins |
| **Length:** | 12.4km |
| **Map:** | Cartes IGN Série Bleue 1837 Ouest Eymet 1:25,000 |
| **Depart from:** | In front of the school in Flaugeac |
| **Signposting:** | Good – new signposts and posts with yellow splashes |

A peaceful walk in the undulating Périgord countryside passing through sleepy hamlets and two small villages, with sweeping views of fields and vineyards.

### How to get there (from Bergerac)
Take the D933, direction Eymet/Marmande, for 13km and then turn left onto the D15 into the hamlet of Flaugeac and turn left in front of the church to reach the *mairie* and school on the left. Park in front of the school by a fence.

### Directions

1    Walk north (away from the village) on the C206 and a few minutes later straight over a crossroads (the C203). Here you see your first wooden post with a yellow splash. There are sweeping views of big fields and woods in all directions with the occasional building.

2    Shortly after the crossroads bear left on a grassy path, passing the cemetery down on the right and a solitary family tomb on the left. The path continues, slightly raised, with a ditch on the left and vineyards on the right to reach a road at a corner (20 mins).

3    Continue straight on the road **(note – if you go right on the road here you will shortly reach the hamlet of Maurillac, which is a shortcut if you wish to take it)**. Where the road turns to the left to a house (Le Caillou), go straight ahead on a track between vines. At the end of the vineyard take the central sunken path (yellow post on the right) going through and round

203

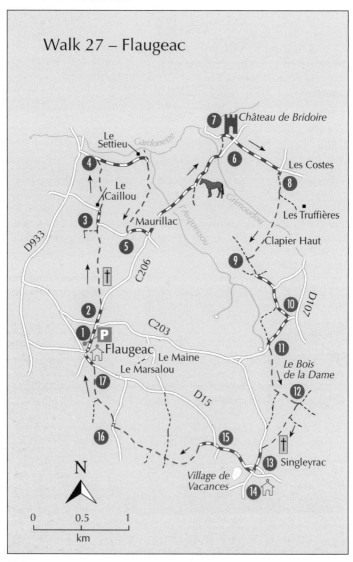

Walk 27 – Flaugeac

Château de Bridoire
7

Le Settieu
4
Gardonette

6
Les Costes
8

Le Caillou
3
Maurillac
5
C206
l'Auguessou
Grimoudou
Les Truffières

Clapier Haut
9

D933

2
10
D107

1 P
Flaugeac
C203
Le Maine
Le Marsalou
11

Le Bois
de la Dame
12

17
D15
15
13 Singleyrac
16
Village de
Vacances
14

N

0        0.5        1
km

the edge of attractive woodland to reach another narrow road and wooden signposts.

4   Turn right, direction Château de Bridoire 3.8km, and continue along the side of an attractive shallow, wooded valley with La Gardonnette stream running through it, and past a house on the right and a larger house on the left, called Le Settieu, to reach a T-junction immediately after. The track goes right and continues along through the side of the wooded valley into open fields and then between two fences to the road you reached at point 3, above (50 mins).

5   Turn left past the Manoir de Maurillac on the left, and shortly afterwards reach a crossroads where you turn left again, signposted La Jumenterie/Roussignac/Bridoire. The road goes down and then up past the Equestrian Centre of La Jumenterie on the right, where you get your first view of the many turrets of the château down on the left, partially hidden in trees and undergrowth. The road goes down and crosses the Grimoudou stream.

6   Immediately after, bear left on a grassy jeep track that is a shortcut to the château, which is hidden in undergrowth and totally abandoned (1hr 30 mins).

*Chat de Bridoire*

Nearby is a placard explaining the curious and rather sad history of this château, which from the outside looks enormous. Built originally in the 15th century but restored in the 19th, it was inhabited from 1806 to 1938 by a family called Foucauld. It was purchased about 20 years ago by a society in Senegal which has since disappeared and all communications sent to them have merely been returned. Since then it has been ransacked and all the furniture burnt or destroyed. At various times renovations have been started and mysteriously discontinued. The state wants to take it over and renovate, but does not seem to make any progress with legal obstacles connected with the original sale. Meanwhile this beautiful château is slowly falling into disrepair. **Note: you join the GR6 briefly from the château to the hamlet of Les Costes, but always follow the posts with yellow splashes.**

7   With the château facing you turn right and, passing a rather worn, sad statue of the Virgin Mary to the right, you shortly come to a small cross-roads. Go straight on, direction Les Costes, upwards to the hamlet. This is a curious little place in that there are a number of houses but no church, square or central point.

8   Walk straight through the hamlet, and immediately after the houses at a small crossroads go down to the right and then left after 100m, where there is a faded yellow mark on a tree. This path goes into a shallow valley of large fields sweeping down to a bush-lined narrow stream. Do not turn left on another jeep track that goes to Les Truffières, but continue downwards to reach a very bushy narrow path (you can skirt this by keeping to the edge of the field on the left) and cross the stream at a bridge. The track goes gradually upwards through wide-open fields to reach a more defined jeep track at the top (2hrs).

9   Turn left to walk into the hamlet of Clapier Haut, passing another solitary family tomb on the left. Walk through the hamlet and bear right at a fork. Continue down the road to reach a T-junction (yellow post).

10  Turn right (the D107 is over on the left) and go down the gently descending road.

11  **Careful** – just before a pond on the right turn off left onto a wide track. Walk past a sign saying that the wood to your left is Le Bois de la Dame and continue. At a fork as the track starts to go up, turn left along a grassy path (yellow post) to reach a crossroad of tracks and signposts.

**12** Turn right, direction Bourg de Singleyrac 0.8km (yellow post), passing a cemetery on the left to reach a T-junction.

**13** Turn left into the village to reach the square and church (2hrs 45 mins). *Singleyrac is a village which has been completely renovated – everything including the* mairie *and church has been cleaned and spruced up. There is a Village Vacances here and a large lake with holiday houses nearby. Personally, I feel that in the process it seems to have lost its soul!* Look for the signs at the side of the information board in the square and follow the sign 'Liaison Flaugeac 2.6km' down the hill to the D15, crossroads and more wooden signs.

**14** Turn right, direction Flaugeac, and go along the D15 for a few minutes, passing the lake and Village Vacances over on the left and vineyards to the right.

**15** Bear left off the road at Chez Cinquet (yellow post) when the D15 bends to the right. After two houses the road turns into a grassy jeep track leading into a sunken lane and into woodland. Follow the track through the wood following the posts and ignore any turnings off. In the middle of the wood there are more wooden signs at a junction – follow sign 'Flaugeac 1.5km'. The track comes out of the woods where there is a lovely open view to the right, including the hamlets of Le Marselou and Le Maine.

**16** The track reaches another road where you turn right briefly and then left by a new house, which is not on the map (yellow post). Keep to the left of the house on a track going through vineyards and then fields. You can see the church of Flaugeac ahead and there are wonderful panoramic views over to the right. Follow the track and posts to arrive at the D15 again.

**17** Turn left into Flaugeac and right in front of the church to reach your car (3hrs 40 mins).

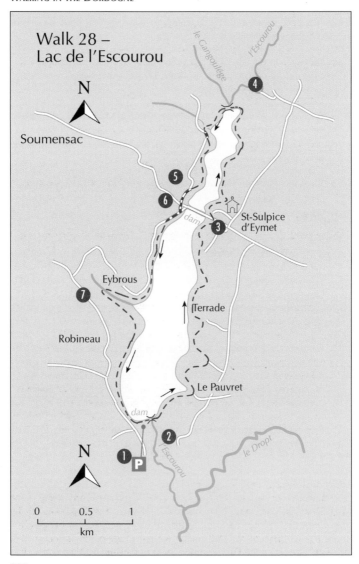

Walk 28 –
Lac de l'Escourou

N

Soumensac

le Gangoulège

l'Escourou

**4**

**5**

**6**

dam

**3**

St-Sulpice
d'Eymet

Eybrous

**7**

Terrade

Robineau

Le Pauvret

dam

**1** P

**2**

l'Escourou

le Dropt

N

0        0.5        1
km

# WALK 28
## *Round the Lac de L'Escourou*

| | |
|---|---|
| **Difficulty:** | A very easy walk round a pretty lake |
| **Time:** | 2hrs plus visit of the *bastide* town of Eymet |
| | Market day Thursday – early closing Wednesday |
| **Length:** | 8.9km |
| **Maps:** | Cartes IGN Série Bleue 1737 East Duras and 1837 Ouest |
| | Eymet. **Note** – the lake is so recent that it does not appear on |
| | the maps |
| **Depart from:** | Parking by the lake |
| **Signposting:** | Some signs plus some posts with yellow splashes, but the way |
| | round is obvious |

This is an attractive man-made lake covering 120 hectares, constructed in 1996 for irrigation reasons. The only leisure activities allowed in the vicinity are fishing, picnicking (there are wooden benches and tables) and the 7km walk around the lake. The walk is extremely pleasant, as the lake has been cleverly landscaped with plantations of young trees interspersed with fields that are covered with wild flowers in springtime. Do not go on a very hot day as, until the young trees grow, there is little shade.

It is worth visiting the *bastide* village of Eymet either before or after the walk. Less well known than the other *bastides* (although 10,000 tourists visit it per year), it is very pretty, with arcades and medieval houses around a central square, and a semi-ruined 13th-century tower and castle. Eymet was founded in the 1270 by Alphonse de Poitiers and changed hands many times during the Hundred Years' War. It later joined Bergerac in its Protestant affiliations.

### How to get there (from Bergerac)
Take the D933 until you see the sign 'Eymet'. Continue on the road over the Dropt river. Shortly after, take a right turn on the D25 signposted Ste-Foy-la-Grande. The road passes the medieval castle and church as you curl round the medieval centre to the left. Turn right on the D18 and cross the river again. Almost immediately, at a fork, turn left on the D25, direction Sauvetat du Drompt. After 4km look for

*Facade house in main square, Eymet*

a turn right to Soumensac/Lac de l'Escourou. Park in the car park on the right below the dam.

## Directions

1    Take the wide track at the end of the car park between two large notice boards. Shortly after, turn left on a narrower track, going up to the dam and wooden signposts. Go right, direction St-Sulpice d'Eymet, on a path along the dam wall, from where you can see the second dam further up, which cuts the lake in two. Cross a bridge at the end over a concrete overflow into the Escourou Rau (*rau* meaning 'small stream') (10 mins).

2    Turn left onto a wide, grassy track and walk along with the lake on the left. The track bends round to the left, passing another parking area on a road coming in from the hamlet of Le Pauvert. Shortly afterwards you see a road on the right which stops at the lake edge. *These are roads which traversed the area before the lake was constructed.* To the right are meadows covered in wild flowers and orchids in springtime. Ahead you can see the hamlet of Terrade. Some of the time there is a wooden fence between the path and the lake, and it seems such a shame that no swimming is allowed as there are little sandy beaches. A second road comes in from the right, stopping before it reaches the lake edge. You are approaching the second dam near the hamlet of St-Sulpice d'Eymet, which you cannot see from the path. *On this track we saw a strange-looking animal with a long tail trotting along in front of us. At first we thought it was a dog or a cat, but on approaching we saw that it was a coypu (see 'Wildlife' in Introduction).* Where the track bears right take a small shortcut left across a grassy dip and then across the road going towards the dam on the left, to reach the car park opposite (50 mins).

3    Cross the car park (post with yellow splash) and continue.

### Diversion

There is a sign up right indicating 12th-century church. This is a narrow wooded path going up fairly steeply to reach a road with a notice board showing a map of the region. The small church is opposite – it has the usual wall tower with a bell in the centre, characteristic of the region. Like most other churches it is usually locked, so you cannot visit the interior.

Lac d'Escourou

When the author did this walk in mid-May huge fish were jumping out of the water and creating quite a noise – these, we were told, were carp catching flies. Continue on towards the upper part of the lake, which is marshy and bordered by yellow flowering irises in May.

4   As you round the top of the lake you cross a small stream (L'Escourou) beside a wooden bridge, now not needed as the water has been piped here and there is a path alongside. Continue round the other side of the lake, where there is also a wooden fence, to arrive at another car park on the other side of the central dam (1hr 5 mins).

5   Cross over the dam and keep straight (the road coming in from the right goes to Soumensac – *a village worth visiting for its extensive views. One of the old villagers told me that on a clear day you can see the Pyrenees!* There is a small lake to the right at this junction (1hr 20 mins).

6   Walk along the road for 180m and then turn left on a grassy track which meanders along the side of the lake. Ignore a path right sign-posted 'Eybrous'.

7   The path does a U-turn left to cross the Ruisseau de Roche, a pleasant spot where there are a number of ducks. This is a good place for a picnic as there is a strategic bench! Continue on the track, passing the hamlet of Roubineau up on the right where you can see the wooden tobacco drying sheds with the doors in the side to let the air circulate through the structure. The path reaches the first dam, where you retrace your steps to the car park (2hrs).

# WALK 29
## *Around Monestier*

| | |
|---|---|
| **Difficulty:** | Medium, as it is fairly long if you do the full double-circuit |
| **Time:** | 4hrs 20 mins |
| **Length:** | 14.6km (2 separate walks of 7km and 5km) with a connecting path between them |
| **Map:** | Cartes IGN Série Bleue 1737 Est Duras 1:25,000. The map is not very useful as some of the paths are not marked. |
| **Depart from:** | In front of the church in Monestier |
| **Signposting:** | This walk is a slight navigating challenge – there are signposts with yellow arrows/splashes and signposts with green arrows/splashes, but not always in the places where you need them most, so follow directions carefully. |

If you want a long but easy itinerary with no great ups and downs, through numerous vineyards, woodland, open fields and shallow valleys, then this is the walk for you! There are no dramatic landmarks on the way around and little habitation – above all, practically no road walking, which is a bonus. You are really in unspoilt Périgord countryside. The itinerary combines two separate walks of 7 and 5km which could be done individually if wanted. There is a connecting path, which has to be done twice (indicated by posts with green splashes).

### How to get there (from Bergerac)
Take the D936, direction Bordeaux, for 13km and at Gardonne turn left on the D4. After 7km turn left again on the D4E, direction Monestier 1km. Park in front of the church where there is an information board showing the walks.

### Directions

1   Walk out of the parking with the church on the left and the Foyer Municipale on the right to reach the D4E at an intersection. Turn right and then left on a bridge over the Merlan stream, direction La Bastide (D16).

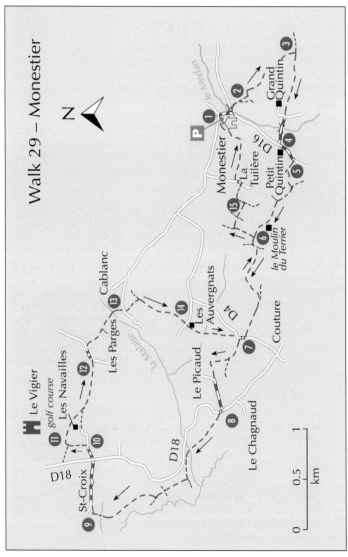

Walk 29 – Monestier

**2**  Take the second turning right between two houses (there are no indications) onto a sunken, grassy path. It bends to the left and then right through vineyards (here you get your first post with yellow splashes). You are rising gently, and if you look behind there is a good view of Monestier. The path goes into a small wood and then into vineyards, continuing uphill through open country. Keep to the lower side of a bank to reach a T-junction where there is a wooden signpost (20 mins).

**3**  Turn right (left is the liaison path between Thenac/Cuneges) and walk through the vines, going gently left and then bearing right towards a farm called Grand Quintin. Continue straight past a farm building with big wine vats inside to reach a small crossroads. Go straight on a narrow road going down and up, crossing a bridge to reach the D16 at Petit Quintin (35 mins).

**4**  Go left and then after 200m go right (**careful** – the yellow arrow on a telephone pole indicates right, but the turning is after the next telephone pole) on a grassy, overgrown track going slightly upwards.

**5**  **Careful** – just before a vineyard on the right (there is a post here but it is not easy to see), go left into woods and then out again. With the vines on your left continue along the side of the trees for a few minutes before you go back into the forest, right. There is a sign here saying 'Palombier – Pigeons libre'. Follow the path past a pigeon hide high in the trees on the left. (**Careful** – go straight here and not left). The path goes into the open again later (post here). Go slightly left and then right to continue upwards through vast vineyards towards a slight rise with a clump of trees and a ruin (on the map this is le Moulin du Terrier). At the top here there are extended views all around.

**6**  Continue downwards, noting a path to the right. **This is the way you will take on your return. You are now entering the liaison path between the two walks, so look for posts with green splashes instead of yellow.** Turn left and after about 100m turn right between vineyards (look carefully for the posts). Go down here and slightly right by a pine tree (post) into bushy woodland. The path through the woods goes left and then zigzags right and left; after this **be careful** to turn right at a T-junction, passing a pigeon hide on the right. When finally emerging from the woods, continue straight through some vines to a T-junction at the D4 road where there is a wooden sign (1hr 20 mins).

**7**   Turn right on the road for around 80m and then turn left into bushy wood-land. **At this point the liaison route finishes and you are now again following yellow splashes. Straight ahead is another post where you will come in on your return.** Turn right at the end of the woods and head down through the vineyards towards a large, beautiful house (Le Picaud on the map). At the end of the vineyards turn left to reach a driveway, with an smaller old house surrounded by a wall on the right. Continue on the track, which becomes paved and reaches the D18 at a T-junction (1hr 45 mins).

**8**   Turn right and then almost immediately left just before a corner (post). There is a large field on the right before the path goes into woodland, bears down into a shallow valley and crosses a stream at the bottom, where there are fields again. You can hear the occasional car on the D18 road nearby on the right as you climb up again, in and out of mixed wood-land. Go along a flattish path, which falls away on the left. **Be careful** – after walking between some tall pines, to turn 90 degrees right at a junc-tion, there is a yellow post – but only after you have turned! You are again walking along a flattish path, which falls away on the left but more abrupt-ly this time. *In these woods in early May, we saw a number of pyramid and lady orchids.*

Go straight ahead at a crossroads in the woods (there is a cross saying not to go right), and then watch **very carefully** for a junction to the right a few minutes later; once again there is a yellow post, but concealed on the left a full 80m after you have turned! The path bears left and goes slightly downhill into a clearing, and then over a culvert into an overgrown mead-ow. Keep to the left on the edge of the meadow as you go up towards the hamlet of Ste-Croix to reach a narrow road (2hrs 25 mins).

**9**   Go right passing a notice saying 'Eglise and accueil' ('church and wel-come'). *This is puzzling as there is no church indicated on the map and the place looks like a house and meeting centre. On reaching the road the puzzle is solved as there is a sign saying 'Centre Ste-Croix, Eglise Orthodoxe'.* Continue on the narrow road (there is a field to the right and vines to the left), crossing the wider D18 road and continuing for a few minutes in the direction of Les Navailles.

**10** **Careful** – look for a post and go left through the vines by two isolated oak trees, towards a large house which, as you get nearer, is revealed as a very up-market golf club. *The links are beautifully mown and people walk* *around in smart golf clothes or dash by in golf buggies. You can see an attractive lake with a row of wooden chalets near the imposing club house (says Château la Vigier on the map) – all rather surprising to find while walking through such a rural and unpopulated area!*

**11** Turn right on a grassy track just before you get to the road leading to the golf cub (no post here). There are vines on the right and only a hedge to the left separating you from the green lawns and golf players. After the vines there is a field on the right, sweeping up to a large, rickety building which is Les Navailles. The path goes into woodland and bears right away from the golf course at a crossing (yellow post), heading up steadily to another road (2hrs 55 mins).

**12** Turn left on the road (post) for 200m, and then right again off the road (well signed) into woodland and out again, passing the rather derelict buildings of Les Parges on the right. Descend gently by fields, vineyards and hedges into another wide, shallow valley, crossing the Ruisseau de la Malaise at a culvert, with the farm of Cablanc on the left, to arrive at a road.

*Small Dordogne manor house surrounded by a protective wall, near Monestier*

**13** Go right for a few metres and then up left (yellow splash on telephone pole) on a grassy track through wasteland. Just after the hedge ends on your left, turn right, still on a grassy path which rises gently by a wood on the left. Keep on the obvious path, following yellow posts down again gently through vineyards, and go right at a fork into a sunken track to shortly reach the road again (3hrs 20 mins).

**14** Go straight across the road, down by a farm called Les Auvergnats with turkeys, sheep, horses, a donkey and an enormous billy-goat, and across the Ruisseau des Auvergnats by a reservoir over on the right. Then climb gently again to reach the D4 at a corner; go right onto the road and then leave it again to the left after 80m (3hrs 20 mins). **This is where the second circular walk ends and you go back on the liaison path – follow posts with green splashes between points 7 and 6 on the sketch map, and continue on to point 15 (route described below).**

Go straight through the vineyards, enter the woods and pass a pigeon hide on your left. About 5 minutes later be careful to turn left at a junction, following green posts. After a right–left zigzag followed by a right bend, go slightly up on a narrower path before leaving the wood into vineyards. Keep straight to a T-junction where you turn left and then right after about 100m. A few minutes later look for the left turn at point 6 onto a new path for the homeward stretch. Go down on a grassy sunken path and into vineyards. Keep straight on at the end of vineyards with wood on your right. **Watch carefully** for a turn up to the right (battered signposts with nothing on them, and a yellow post soon after the turn). Continue straight at a crossing with a yellow post over the brow.

**15** At the following T-junction turn left and after a few minutes the path bears right towards a plum orchard and a narrow road leading to a farm on the right called La Tuillère (4hrs 5 mins).

Turn left on the road for a moment and then off to the right – there are vines to the left and plum orchards on the right. The path bends to the left, goes up briefly and then bends to the right round the top of the orchard. Shortly after, you go left into woodland and descend round the side of the wood – you can see the church and the houses of Monestier just ahead. When you reach the village, where small modern houses are being constructed, bear up left to the church and car park (4hrs 20 mins).

# WALK 30
## *St-Georges-de-Montclard*

| | |
|---|---|
| **Difficulty:** | Easy – undulating through woodland |
| **Time:** | 2hrs 30 mins plus 15 mins if you wish to climb the Roc St-Georges |
| **Length:** | 7.9km |
| **Map:** | Cartes IGN Série Bleue 1836 Est Cressye 1:25,000 |
| **Depart from:** | In front of the post office in St-Georges-de-Montclard |
| **Signposting:** | Follow the posts with yellow splashes except where indicated otherwise |

A pleasant walk from one of the prettiest villages north of Bergerac – the name St-Georges-de-Montclard is also spelt St-Georges-de-Montclar (without the d) depending on which way you enter the village! To complicate things further, according to the IGN map St-Georges-de-Montclard is a *commune* (parish) consisting of the village of Montclard and the nearby hamlet of St-Georges. So why the sign to St-Georges-de-Montclard? There is quite a lot of walking in woodland, mainly chestnut woods, so this is especially appropriate for a hot, sunny day. It is worth strolling round the village and reading the inscriptions on the old buildings – the covered market was reconstructed in 1655 and restored in 1840. It was used once a month as a market place until 1945. It is interesting to note that the tethered cattle licked the stone pillars for the salt. The small fortified château, built in the 11th century on an artificial mound (motte), has been reconstructed many times and was partially destroyed in the Revolution. For some time in the 1800s it was used as a quarry and was last restored in 1994. It is now privately owned. There is also a row of ancient houses which has been turned into a Protestant church. You can also climb the Roc St-Georges before or after your walk (see directions below).

**Note:** Every Friday evening in July and August there is a village fête, and parking is not permitted in the centre of the village after 16.00hrs.

### How to get there (from Bergerac)
Take the N21, direction Perigeux. Some 2km after the village of Lembras turn off right on the D21E (loses the E after a few km!), signposted Lamonzie-Montastruc

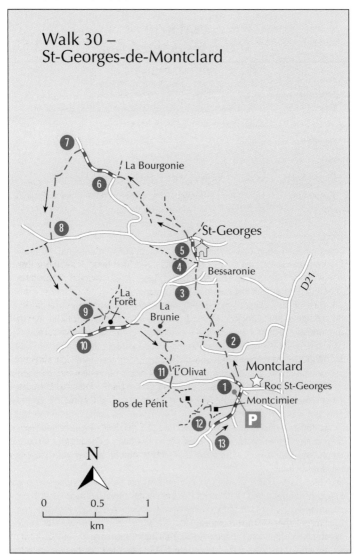

# Walk 30 –
# St-Georges-de-Montclard

La Bourgonie

St-Georges

Bessaronie

La Forêt

La Brunie

Montclard

Roc St-Georges

Montcimier

L'Olivat

Bos de Pénit

D21

N

0    0.5    1
km

### To climb the Roc St-Georges

After the sign St-Georges-de-Montclard turn left and then go into a parking area to the right where there is a notice board with a map of the area and the walk you will be doing. Turn right out of the parking area and up some steps on to a narrow path, right, just before the gates of the village school. This is a medium-steep climb of about 5 mins to reach a small, grassy plateau where there is an overhanging rock to the left – there is also a sign saying you are looking at the Caudeau valley. Follow an undefined path left to climb up the rock from the back, where the view is even more extensive.

and Vergt. Continue along this road for 10km till you see the sign to St-Georges-de-Montclard. Shortly after, turn left towards the centre of the village and park in front of the post office near the old covered market place (18km from Bergerac).

### Directions

1   Walk out of the village, direction Campsegret (northwest) – there is a sign in front of the post office so you can't go wrong! Around 100m later (yellow splash on a tree), turn up right after the last house on a wide, grassy track bordered by a stone wall which climbs steeply out of the village (10 mins). **Note**: This walk is also a nature trail, and from time to time you will see a wooden sign indicating the type of tree alongside.

2   At the top go straight across a narrow road, where there is a sign 'Chemin pedestre', and skirt a large field before going into beech and chestnut woods. At a T-junction bear right and continue gently downwards across a crossroads in the woods to arrive at a narrow road (20 mins).

3   Following yellow arrows cross the road and go down a narrow, sunken, grassy path (you can divert, right, to the hamlet of Bessaronie to see a couple of lovely old houses) to reach a further narrow road a few minutes later.

4   Turn right (there is a statue of the Virgin Mary at this corner) and then immediately turn left onto a wider paved road and walk into the attractive hamlet of St-Georges (ignore road coming in left). There is a sign by a stream saying 'Lavoir/Moulin' 100m further on the left (an old flourmill which was used to make bread until 1945). Pass the Romanesque church

*Ancient covered market,
St-Georges-de-Montclard*

of St-George, which is dedicated to St-Rita, patron of hopeless causes. *It is worth taking a look inside to see the statue to St-Rita surrounded by fresh flowers (there is a notice saying she doesn't like artificial ones!) and also an 18th-century wooden crucifix.* After the church there is a T-junction (30 mins).

5   Following yellow splashes go left on a narrow road through the hamlet and then turn right up a jeep track between two houses. This is a raised track with a steep bank to the right and fields down on the left. Where the track bends to the left, go straight on a grassy track (you do not see a yellow splash till later) and continue on this flat path through attractive woods and glades ignoring any other paths coming in. You reach a sign by a spring (now a dirty patch of water surrounded by concrete and stinging nettles). This is the Fontaine des Léberous (*léberous* must be a local word) and the sign recounts a charming legend:

*Léberous were men who came to the fountain and changed into sheep or hares. During the night they raced through seven parishes and passed under seven bell towers. If, when the first cock crowed at dawn, they had not returned to the fountain they stayed as sheep or hares for evermore!*

There is a wooden table and benches at this spot, which is a nice place for a picnic (once you have beaten down the nettles).

Continue through light woodland and fields to meet a denser wood where the ground is covered in ivy. Following yellow splashes turn right steeply up to a narrow road at La Bourgonie (50 mins).

6　Turn right up a narrow road back into chestnut forest, past a small, ugly reservoir building on the left, after which there is a field to the right.

7　**Careful** – look for a turning left (yellow splash) onto a jeep track which goes down into light chestnut woods where there is lots of bracken. The track goes down skirting a shallow valley with a field on the left and then goes up again. There is a sign indicating that this is the site of a former *four à charbon* which was used until 1945; the machine turned charcoal into fuel for vehicles that functioned on gazogene (gas generators). The track undulates along to reach another junction (1hr 15 mins).

8　Go right then left (entrance to a lovely house) and immediately left again (no yellow splash at the turning). Keep to the main grassy track down into forest again, passing another sign indicating that 'In Roman times there were iron mines in the region, the iron being forged into cannon balls. During the lst World War the residue was used for reforging in the nearby village of Fumel.'

*Hamlet of St-Georges*

*11th-century fortified château, St-Georges-de-Montclard*

**9** Go right at a junction in the woods near a small, hidden cottage called La Forêt. Shortly after go left at a fork to reach a road (1hr 35 mins).

**10** Go left for about 10 mins and then turn right just before a crossroads (well indicated by yellow splashes) onto a jeep track passing a house on the right. Keep on the main track that starts to descend to another shallow valley and the road to St-Georges-de-Montclard (2hrs) – **here you can turn left and walk into the village by the road**.

**11** Cross over the road and take direction Bos de Pénit, passing a large building which looks like a meeting place of some kind (called L'Olivat on the map). The road bears right in front of a house by two huge old firs and a small muddy lake (there is also a swimming pool). Follow the jeep track into woods, ignoring the first undefined track to the left.

**12** **Careful** – as the track bends to the right where the yellow splashes continue, take a narrow path to the left (not very defined but by a large fir tree) to reach a house at Montcimier. Go left on a stony jeep track towards the front entrance of a large white house with a muddy pond and tower to the left (the house has a colonial style and is untypical of the region – the author was told that Sarah Bernhardt was a frequent visitor). Turn right in front of the house down a lane to reach a road (2hrs 15 mins).

**13** Turn left to reach the village (2hrs 30 mins).

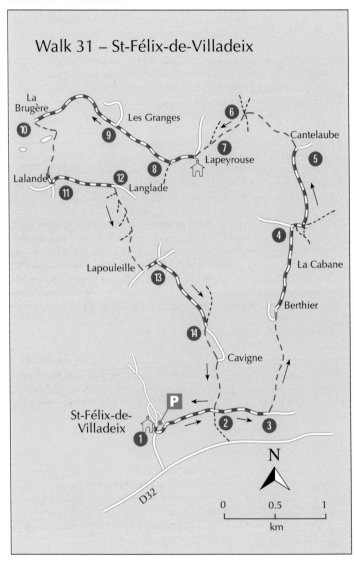

Walk 31 – St-Félix-de-Villadeix

La Brugère

Les Granges

10

9

Cantelaube

6

7 Lapeyrouse

5

8

Lalande

12 Langlade

11

4

La Cabane

Lapouleille

13

Berthier

14

Cavigne

P

St-Félix-de-Villadeix

1

2

3

N

D32

0    0.5    1
km

# WALK 31
## *St-Félix-de-Villadeix*

| | |
|---|---|
| **Difficulty:** | Easy, undulating walk |
| **Time:** | 3hrs 15 mins |
| **Length:** | 12.2km |
| **Map:** | Cartes IGN Série Bleue 1836 Est Creysse 1:25,000 |
| **Depart from:** | By the side of the church in the village of St-Félix-de-Villadeix |
| **Signposting:** | Follow posts with yellow splashes – sometimes not obvious |

A really satisfying walk around the rolling countryside north of Bergerac with lots of sweeping views in all directions, as some of the time you are walking on high ground. The huge green fields planted with barley, winter wheat, maize and sunflowers are fascinating shades of green, mingled with the brown stony soil of the ploughed fields. It is worthwhile visiting the Motte Féodale ('feudal mount'), 2km from St-Félix, at the end of the walk. St-Félix-de-Villadeix is a lovely, unpretentious hamlet with a 'far from the madding crowd' feel about it, even though it is not far from Bergerac.

### How to get there (from Bergerac)
Take the D660, direction Lalinde, through Creysse and turn left onto the D21, direction St-Sauveur, just before Mouleydier. Beware – the sign is not visible until you reach the junction. After St-Sauveur turn right on the D32 through Librac-sur-Louyre, and then left to St-Félix-de-Villadeix. Head up right into the village and park next to the church.

### Directions

1   Go past the front of the church and turn immediately left steeply down a narrow road (clear yellow splashes) past a restored *lavoir* (wash trough). Just before you reach a wider road turn left, signposted Garissade, and right soon after. Ignore roads joining and follow yellow splashes along the side of a shallow valley with a high bank to the left. There is the occasional house and a small square water-pumping station right.

Deserted house, near St-Félix-de-Villadeix

**2**   After 12 mins you reach a crossroads. Continue straight on the road (the track coming in from the left is where you come out on your return) going along the valley bottom.

**3**   Just after bearing left round a slight corner, go left into a field on a wide track – cross on road ahead (20 mins). You are going round the right side of a large field with woods on the immediate right and you can hear the sound of water. The track starts to go up gently through a patch of woodland and then into wide-open fields. Keep to the main track with the fields on your right. You reach an elevated area where there are extended views in all directions. Up ahead are the buildings of a farm called Berthier – to the left you can see another group of houses called Cavigne. The track continues upward through the fields, and then between hedges past the rear of the farm on the right. When the track joins a paved road continue on straight past a very attractive renovated house (La Cabane) and then a smaller house that seems to sit at the very top of this high ground. From this spot there are lovely views of rolling fields and woods in all directions. Shortly afterwards you reach a road at a T-junction with fields on both sides (50 mins).

**4**   Turn right onto the road into woodland. The road swings round to the left (do not go straight on the jeep track) and continues though fields and into woods again before bending right into the hamlet of Cantelaube, dominated by a beautiful house ringed with a dense, high box hedge.

5   **Careful, no yellow splash here**. Go left before the gates of the house and cross a sort of mowed village green (you can see the stately garden of the house over on the right). The track curls down to the left through trees past a gaggle of ducks and there are beautiful views. Keep to the left (look for yellow splashes) where there are tracks going off right. The way becomes a narrow bushy path as you continue downwards, crossing a tiny stream at the bottom to reach an intersection of five paths. In spring there is an impressive display of wild columbines here (1hr 15 mins).

6   Take the second left (yellow sign saying 'Marche' and a yellow arrow; ignore confusing yellow marks to the right) and continue along the bottom with an embankment to the right and a narrow field through trees to the left, and then steadily up through woodland proper. Ignore a newly made unpaved road up left to a place called 'Village Constant'. *This is a recently built holiday village of small houses, mainly for English tourists.* The path joins a jeep track at an impressive wooden cross with roses and a box-wood hedge round the base (1hr 30 mins).

7   Turn left on the jeep track (beautiful view here) and continue past a neat, small patch of tilled soil planted with orchids – *when the author did this walk she saw bee, fly, butterfly, lizard and pyramid orchids in flower together – a rare and pleasing sight*. Soon afterwards the track meets a paved road (you can see the turrets of a château poking out of the trees on the horizon right). Continue straight into the hamlet of Lapeyrouse, passing a sign saying 'Handicapées, sourds, aveugles' ('handicapped, deaf, blind') and shortly after another 'Frères de St-Gabriel'. There is a large house on the left, which looks like an institution, and further on a small church built in a somewhat Victorian style, next to a small park with a memorial opposite. *This is a Maison de Retraite for elderly members of a Catholic brotherhood who were responsible for a small nursing home for the handicapped, now run by the state.*

8   Shortly after, turn right onto another road signposted 'La Brugère' and 'Les Granges' (yellow splashes). This is a flat road through rolling pastoral country bordered by an occasional house and fruit trees. At Les Granges leave the main road, which turns off to the right.

9   Continue straight on a narrower road (yellow splash), not down left, through scattered woodland where there are some little houses (*clearly a community of Dutch people as there is a sign in Dutch*).

**10**  Go left just before the road turns right to a large house and campsite called La Brugère (2hrs). The track goes down towards a little lake with an island in the middle (*we could see people sunbathing around it and there was a place for swimming*), crosses a wide culvert at the end of the lake and then starts to go up again passing a big field on the left and a chestnut wood to the right to reach a paved road at Lalande, consisting of a few beautifully renovated houses. The road bends to the left and meets another road (2hrs 15 mins).

**11**  Turn left on the road, past an orchard of peach, almond and plum trees, into woodland and then out into the open and into woods again.

**12**  Just after the edge of the chestnut forest turn right by a renovated house (Langlade) on the right and another smaller dilapidated house immediately left, on a wide dirt track down into woods. Ignore a first turning right and then turn left at a fork. At the next junction keep straight along a fence (no yellow splash) and then go left at a further fork. The track continues by a large open field, left, and a wood to the right towards the houses of Lapouleille. Go straight through the houses onto a jeep track to reach a road (2hrs 40 mins).

**13**  Turn left to walk by some smart houses to reach a crossroads. Turn right, signed Le Placiaz Cavigne, and continue on a flat road through woods, clearings and fields, descending gently.

**14**  **Careful** – about 15 mins along the road, look for a sign on a telephone pole indicating a turn right off the road in woodland. This is opposite a track coming in from the left but it is not easy to see and is rather undefined at the start (2hrs 55 mins). The track goes down a sunken path and joins a jeep track on a corner, with a farm on the left (Cavigne). Go straight on, past a house on the right and down another sunken, overgrown path. It passes an open area on the left where you can see the sweep of fields up to the high route walked earlier, with the buildings of Berthier on the horizon. The path continues downwards on an old mule trail with overgrown walls each side, and then bushes, to reach the original road at point 2 (see above). Retrace your steps to the church (3hrs 15 mins).

# APPENDIX A:
## Maps

The maps referred to in this guide are at a scale of 1:25,000 (1cm: 250m), as these show the paths clearly.

**Note** – many of the maps, especially in the Bergerac area, are the old Série Bleue maps, originally printed in 1971 (although many have been updated since). These maps do not show the walking paths, which makes them rather difficult to use. They are slowly being replaced by the more legible IGN Top 25 series.

### Sarlat area
Cartes IGN Série Bleue 2035 Ouest Montignac/Grotte de Lascaux (walk 1)
Cartes IGN 2036 ET Top 25 Sarlat/Souillac/Vallée de la Dordogne
(walks 2, 3, 4, 9, 11)
Cartes IGN 1936 ET Top 25 Les Eyzies/Vallées de la Dordogne et de la Vézère
(walks 5, 6, 7, 8)
Cartes IGN Série Bleue 2037 Ouest Domme (walks 7, 10)
Cartes IGN 2136 ET Top 25 Rocamadour/Padirac/Vallée de la Dordogne
(walks 12, 13, 14, 15)
Cartes IGN Série Bleue 2037 Est Gourdon (walk 16)

### Bergerac area
Cartes IGN Série Bleue 1936 Ouest Lalinde (walks 17, 18, 19)
Cartes IGN Série Bleue 1836 Est Creysse (walks 20, 30, 31)
Cartes IGN Série Bleue 1837 Est Castillonnès (walks 20, 23, 24, 25)
Cartes IGN Série Bleue 1937 Ouest Beaumont (Dordogne) (walks 21, 22)
Cartes IGN Série Bleue 1837 Ouest Eymet (walks 26, 27, 28)
Cartes IGN Série Bleue 1737 Est Duras (walks 28, 29)
Cartes IGN Série Bleue 1937 Est Belvès (walk 21)
Cartes IGN Série Bleue 1938 Monflanquin (walk 21)

### Maps 1:100,000 (1cm: 1km)
IGN Top 100 No.48 Périgueux/Tulle (Sarlat area)
IGN Top 100 No.57 Cahors/Montaubon (south Sarlat)
IGN Top 100 No.47 Périgueux (Bergerac area)
IGN Top 100 No.56 Marmande (south Bergerac)

## Useful maps showing whole area
Carte Michelin 1:200,000 Bordeaux/Périgueux/Tulle
Cartes IGN 1:140,000 No.24 Dordogne

The above maps should be available in larger bookshops with a travel section or they can be ordered from specialist shops below.

## Specialist shops
**Stanfords**          12–14 Long Acre, Convent Garden, London WC2E 9LP.
Tel:                   020 7836 1321
Fax:                   020 7836 0189
Website:               www.stanfords.co.uk
Stanfords have the largest selection of guides and maps in England. Anything they do not have in stock can be ordered (delivery 2–4 weeks).

**The Map Shop**       15 High Street, Upton-upon-Severn, Worcs WR8 OHJ
Tel:                   01684 593146 (Freephone: 0800 085 4080)
Fax:                   01684 594559
Email:                 themapshop@btinternet.com
Website:               www.themapshop.co.uk

Websites where IGN maps can be ordered and sent:
                       www.map-world.co.uk
                       www.maps2anywhere.com
                       www.ign.fr (this is the official French IGN website)

Local newsagents and bookshops in the Dordogne sell maps and guidebooks (the latter mainly in French). The big supermarket chains in most towns also stock local maps (often cheaper).

# APPENDIX B:
## Tourist Offices and Syndicats d'Initiative

Many of these Tourist Offices speak English and/or have English documentation. When phoning from outside France the prefix is 0033 + 9 digits (omit first zero).

**For general information on the Dordogne *département***
Comité Départemental du Tourisme de la Dordogne
25 Rue du Président-Wilson, B.P.2063
24002 Périgueux Cedex
Tel:        05.53.35.50.24 and 05.53.35.50.30
Fax:       05.53.09.51.41
Email:    dordogne.perigord.tourisme@wanadoo.fr
Internet: www.perigord.tm.fr/tourisme/cdt
Open:    8.30–12.30/13.30–17.00.

**For general information on the Lot *département***
Comité Départemental du Tourisme du Lot
107 Quai Eugène Cavignac, 46001 Cahors
Tel:        05.65.35.07.09
Fax:       05.65.23.92.76
Email:    le-lot@wanadoo.fr
Internet: www.tourisme-lot.com

**Tourist Offices and Syndicat d'Initiatives in the Bergerac region (Périgord Poupre) applicable to the walks in the book**
**Note:**    OT:        Office de Tourisme (the stars indicate how important it is)
                SI:         Syndicat d'Initiative, which usually has less information

**Beaumont 2440: OT\***
Tel:        05.53.22.39.12
Fax:       05.53.22.05.35
Email:    ot.beaumont@wanadoo.fr
Internet: www.pays-des-bastides.com

**Bergerac 24100: OT\*\***
Tel:       05.53.57.03.11
Fax:       05.53.61.11.04
Email:     tourisme-bergerac@aquinet.tm.fr
Internet:  www.bergerac-tourisme.com

**Creysse 24100: SI**
Tel/Fax:   05.53.23.20.45
Email:     port-de-creysse@wanadoo.fr
Internet:  perigord.tm.fr/servtourisme/otsi/creysse

**Eymet 24500: OT\***
Fax:       05.53.27.98.76
Email:     ot.eymet@perigord.tm.fr
Internet:  www.eymet-en-perigord.com

**Issigeac 24560: SI**
Tel/Fax:   05.53.22.82.71
Email:     si.issegeac@perigord.tm.fr
Internet:  perigord.tm.fr/servtourisme/otsi/issigeac

**Lalinde 24150: OT\***
Tel:       05.53.61.08.55
Fax:       05.53.61.00.64
Email:     ot.lalinde@perigord.tm.fr
Internet:  www.lalinde-perigord.com

**Monpazier 24540: OT\***
Tel:       05.53.22.68.59
Fax:       05.53.74.30.08
Email:     ot.monpazier@perigord.tm.fr
Internet:  www.pays-des-bastides.com

**Tremolat 24510: SI**
Tel:       05.53.22.89.33
Fax:       05.53.22.82.71
Internet:  www.pays-de-Bergerac.com/mairie/tremolat

**Tourist Offices and Syndicat d'Initiatives in the Sarlat region (Périgord Noir) relevant to walks in the book**

**Beynac 24220: OT***
Tel/Fax:    05.53.29.43.08
Email:      info@cc-perigord-noir.fr
Internet:   www.cc-perigord-noir.fr

**Domme 24250: OT***
Tel:        05.53.31.71.00
Fax:        05.53.31.71.09
Email:      domm-tourisme@wanadoo.fr
Internet:   www.domme-tourisme.com

**Eyzies (Les) 24620: OT****
Tel:        05.53.06.97.05
Fax:        05.53.06.90.79
Email:      contact@leseyzies.com
Internet:   www.leseyzies.com

**Montignac 24290: OT***
Tel:        05.53.51.82.60
Fax:        05.53.50.49.72
Email:      ot.montignac@perigord.tm.fr
Internet:   www.bienvenue-montignac.com

**La Roque-Gageac 24250: SI**
Tel:        05.53.29.17.01
Fax:        05.53.31.24.48
Email:      info@cc-perigord-noir.fr
Internet:   www.cc-perigord-noir.fr

**Salignac 24590: SI**
Tel:        05.53.28.81.93
Fax:        05.53.28.85.26
Email:      ot.salignac@perigord.tm.fr
Internet:   perigord.tm.fr/servtourisme/otsi/salignac

**Sarlat 24203: OT\*\*\***

| | |
|---|---|
| Tel: | 05.53.31.45.45 |
| Fax: | 05.53.59.19.44 |
| Email: | info@ot-sarlat-perigord.fr |
| Internet: | www.ot-sarlat-perigord.fr |

**Tourist Offices and Syndicat d'Initiatives in the Lot *département* (walk nos.12, 13, 14, 15 and 16)**

**Gourdon 46500: OT**

| | |
|---|---|
| Tel: | 05.65.27.52.50 |
| Fax: | 05.65.27.52.52 |
| Email: | gourdon@wanadoo.fr |
| Internet: | www.quercy.net/quercy/gourdon |

**Martel 46600: OT**

| | |
|---|---|
| Tel: | 05.65.37.43.44 |
| Fax: | 05.65.37.37.27 |
| Email: | martel2@wanadoo.fr |
| Internet: | www.martel.fr/index.php |

**Padirac 46500: OT**

| | |
|---|---|
| Tel: | 05.65.33.47.17 |
| Fax: | 05.65.33.47.18 |
| Email: | pays-de-padirac@wanadoo.fr |

**Rocamadour 46500: OT\***

| | |
|---|---|
| Tel: | 05.65.33.22.00 |
| Fax: | 05.65.33.22.01 |
| Email: | rocamadour@wanadoo.fr |
| Internet: | www.rocamadour.com |

**Souillac 46200: OT\*\*\***

| | |
|---|---|
| Tel: | 05.65.37.81.56 |
| | 05.65.27.11.45 |
| Email: | office@tourisme-souillac.com |
| Internet: | www.tourisme-souillac.com |

# APPENDIX C:
## Market days

Below is a list of the market days in the towns and villages mentioned in the book. They mainly start early and finish around 13.00. There are three types of market – *marché traditionnel*, which is a normal market offering a wide range of goods and produce; *marché paysan,* where the local farmers sell their home-grown produce; and *marché nocturne,* held in the tourist season and geared to the holiday maker. There are also *foires* in the larger towns, which are trade fairs with a range of farming and industrial equipment. The larger ones include exhibiting and judging livestock, and often have a fairground. Very popular are markets with a theme (also called *foires*), such as Foire aux vins et huitres (wine and oysters), Foire aux bestiaux (animals), Foire aux livres (books), Foire Brocante (bric a brac) and so on. For information regarding these markets telephone the local tourist office.

### Traditional markets in the Périgord Noir (Sarlat area) and Lot (Souillac area)

| | |
|---|---|
| **Monday:** | Les Eysiès, St-Cyprien |
| **Tuesday:** | Salignac-Eyvigues, Gourdon |
| **Wednesday:** | Montignac, Sarlat, Périgueux, Martel |
| **Thursday:** | Domme |
| **Friday:** | Salignac-Eyvigues, Souillac |
| **Saturday:** | Montignac, Périgueux, Sarlat, Martel, Gourdon |
| **Sunday:** | St-Geniès, St-Sozy |

### Périgord Poupre (Bergerac area)

| | |
|---|---|
| **Tuesday:** | Beaumont, Trémolat |
| **Wednesday:** | Bergerac |
| **Thursday:** | Lalinde, Monpazier, Mouleydier, Eymet |
| **Saturday:** | Beaumont, Bergerac |
| **Sunday:** | Couze, Creysse, Issigeac, Singleyrac (July/August only) |

# APPENDIX D:
## *Glossary of Local and Useful Words*

| | |
|---|---|
| Abri | small shelter |
| Aven | or *avenc* (Occitan) – hole or cave caused by erosion in a limestone soil; a swallow hole or sinkhole |
| Bastide | in the Dordogne area, a fortified town built in the 12th century |
| Castiné | unpaved stony road (jeep track) |
| Château | castle |
| Château d'eau | water-tower |
| Cingles | oxbow bends made in the Dordogne river (eg Cingle de Tremolat) |
| Clochers-murs | high wall at the front of the church housing two or three bells – a common feature in southwest France |
| Ecluse | canal lock – see walk no.19 |
| Fontaine | fountain |
| Gabarres | traditional flat-bottomed boats which took goods up and down the Dordogne until the turn of the 20th century |
| Gariotte | small, dry-stone oval shelter (called a *borie* in Provence) – used principally by shepherds |
| Grotte | grotto – underground cave |
| Halle | covered market |

| | |
|---|---|
| Mas | conglomeration of farm buildings housing extended families – formerly self-sufficient |
| Moulin | mill |
| Pech | small hill |
| Pigonnier | dovecot |
| Puy | a low, tree-covered hill (local word) |
| Rau | small stream (local word) |

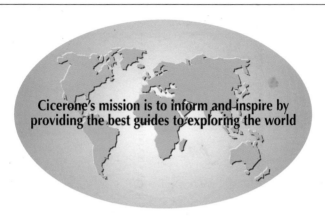

Cicerone's mission is to inform and inspire by providing the best guides to exploring the world

Since its foundation over 30 years ago, Cicerone has specialised in publishing guidebooks and has built a reputation for quality and reliability. It now publishes nearly 300 guides to the major destinations for outdoor enthusiasts, including Europe, UK and the rest of the world.

Written by leading and committed specialists, Cicerone guides are recognised as the most authoritative. They are full of information, maps and illustrations so that the user can plan and complete a successful and safe trip or expedition – be it a long face climb, a walk over Lakeland fells, an alpine traverse, a Himalayan trek or a ramble in the countryside.

With a thorough introduction to assist planning, clear diagrams, maps and colour photographs to illustrate the terrain and route, and accurate and detailed text, Cicerone guides are designed for ease of use and access to the information.

If the facts on the ground change, or there is any aspect of a guide that you think we can improve, we are always delighted to hear from you.

**Cicerone Press**
2 Police Square  Milnthorpe  Cumbria  LA7 7PY
Tel:01539 562 069   Fax:01539 563 417
e-mail:info@cicerone.co.uk   web:www.cicerone.co.uk

**CICERONE**